UPSTAIRS DOWNSTAIRS

UPSTAIRS DOWNSTAIRS

Edited by Aisha Hasanovic

images
Publishing

Published in Australia in 2006 by
The Images Publishing Group Pty Ltd
ABN 89 059 734 431
6 Bastow Place, Mulgrave, Victoria, 3170, Australia
Telephone: +61 3 9561 5544 Facsimilie: +61 3 9561 4860
Email: books@images.com.au
Website: www.imagespublishing.com

National Library of Australia Cataloguing-in-Publication data:

Upstairs downstairs.

Includes index.
ISBN 1 920744 34 7.

1. Stairs - Designs and plans. 2. Staircases - Designs and plans.

721.832

Coordinating Editor: Aisha Hasanovic

Designed by The Graphic Image Studio Pty Ltd, Mulgrave, Australia
www.tgis.com.au

Digital production by Splitting Image Colour Studio Pty Ltd, Australia

Printed by Everbest Printing Co. Ltd, in Hong Kong/China

IMAGES has included on its website a page for special notices
in relation to this and our other publications.
Please visit:
www.imagespublishing.com

FOREWORD

Throughout history, stairs have taken us from one level to the next. In the beginning we piled rocks into simple step forms to access difficult areas on uphill slopes, to make it easier to get back down. As time progressed we moved the stairs indoors, and eventually, stairs housed in a case became a symbol of wealth in the home. The bigger your home, the more stairs you needed—and they were usually ornate and grand.

Today, space is increasingly limited, and we are often required to build up, rather than out. The single-story home or office is rare. *Upstairs Downstairs* is a pictorial exploration of the aesthetic benefits stairs can bring into domestic and commercial spaces, even though, especially in commerce, we are more likely to rely on lifts and escalators to take us up and down.

In this book an array of projects are featured that offer plenty of design ideas for the balustrades, treads, risers, handrails or the full staircase. Stairs can decorate a vertical space, act as a focal point between two floors, and remain functional as well. Stairs can be flush to a wall, or work their way up from the center of a room or building. The possibilities are numerous.

Color photographs show how stairs can slice up an enormous open space for a dramatic visual effect, or how a spiral or elliptical staircase can create a smooth and graceful transition from one level to the next. There are stairs that dominate a room because of the materials they are made from, and there are stairs where color or lighting create something unique and subtle. The designs in *Upstairs Downstairs* are recent: each staircase is different and there is a mixture of both classic and modern styles.

Floor plans, sections, and details accompany most of the stairs in this book for the architect or designer who may want this valuable information. For the lover of design, or the renovator, the beautiful photography will amaze and inspire.

Aisha Hasanovic
Editor

Architect: Barton Myers Associates, Inc.   Photography: Tim Griffith

Architect: Foster and Partners   **Photography:** Nigel Young

and let thy feet
millenniums hence
be set in midst of knowledge

Tennyson

Architect: Goettsch Partners   Photography: Steinkamp/Ballog Photography

11

Architect: Bing Thom Architects   Photography: Nic Lehoux

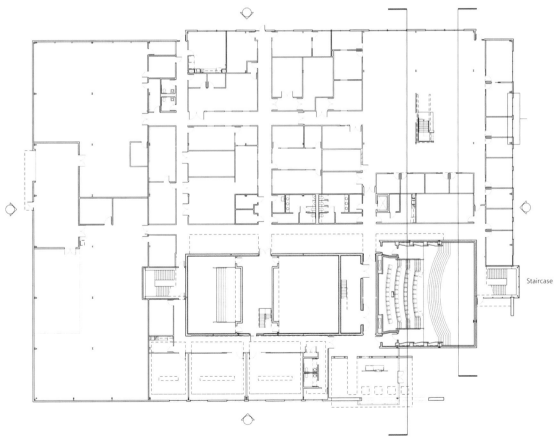

Staircase

Architect: HLW   Photography: J Scott Smith

Architect: Kohn Pedersen Fox Associates   **Photography**: H.G. Esch

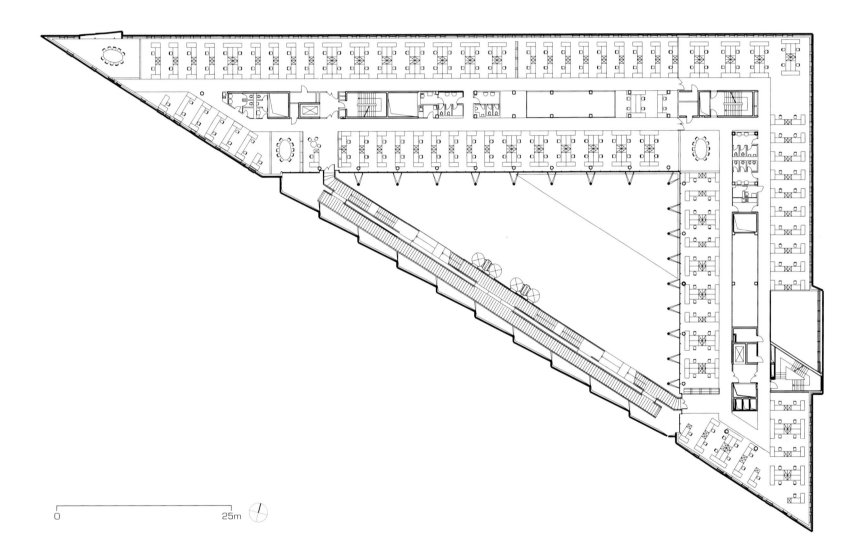

0   25m

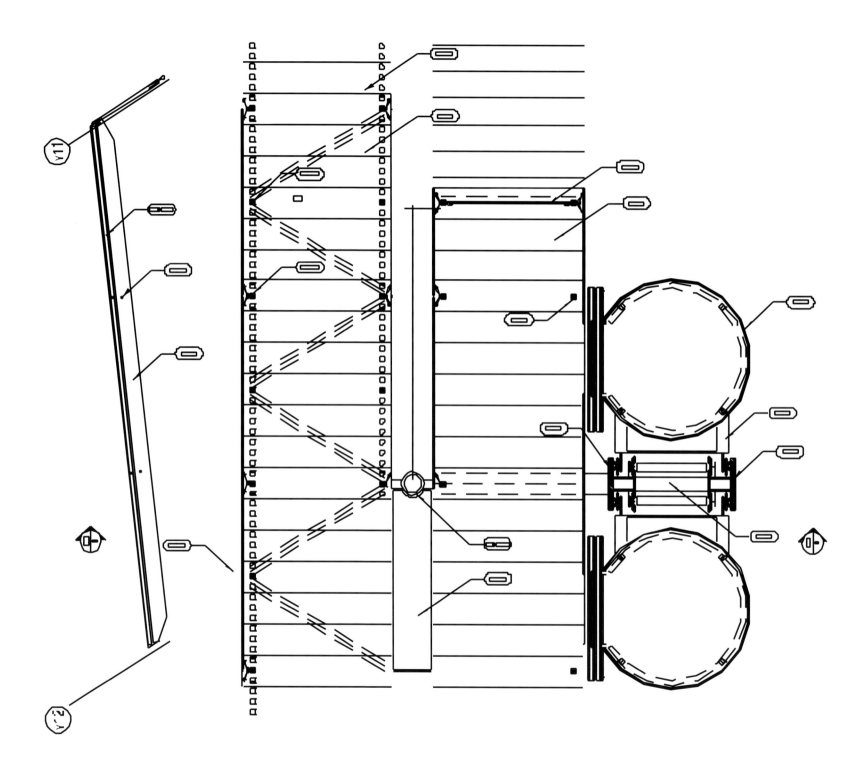

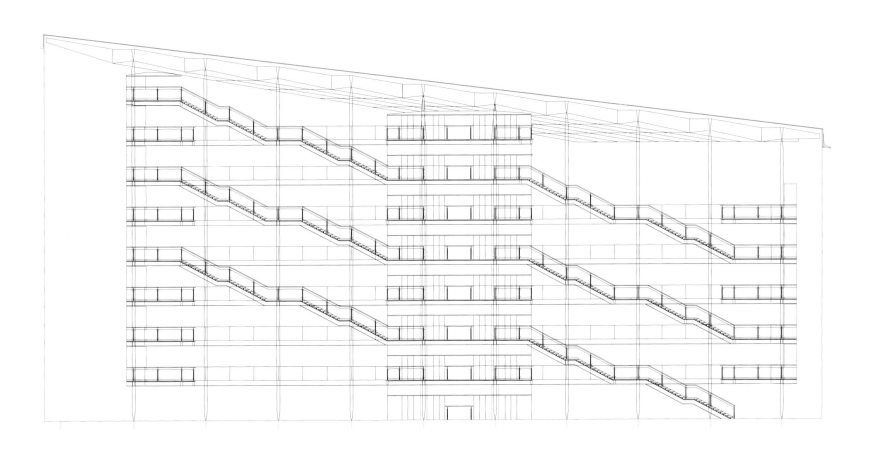

21

Architect: 3XNielsen   Photography: Adam Mørk

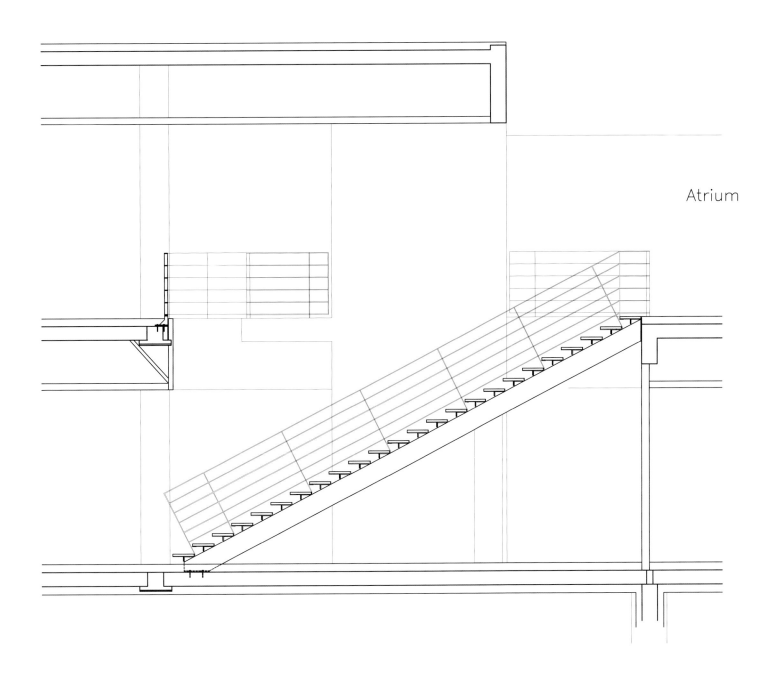

Atrium

Architect: Platt Byard Dovell White   Photography: Johnathan Wallan

Architect: Saucier + Perrotte Architects   **Photography:** Marc Cramer

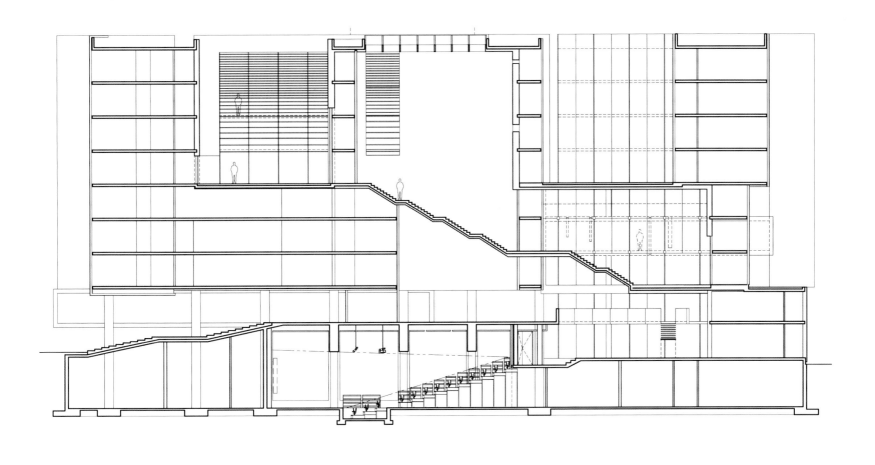

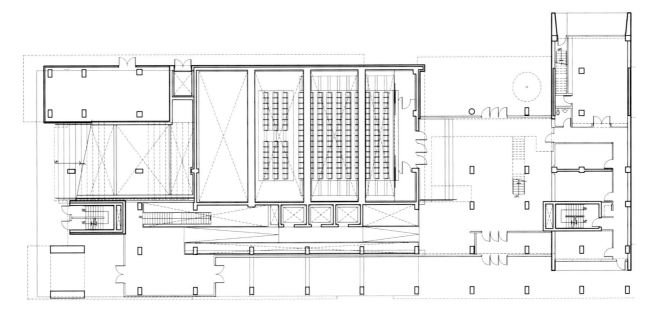

Studio
Study
17.5m2

Zimmer
Room
15.0m2

Zimmer
Room
25.5m2

Zimmer
Room
42.5m2

0   2M

Architect: Camenzind Evolution   **Photography:** Ferit Kuyas

Architect: CCS Architecture   **Photography**: Cesar Rubio

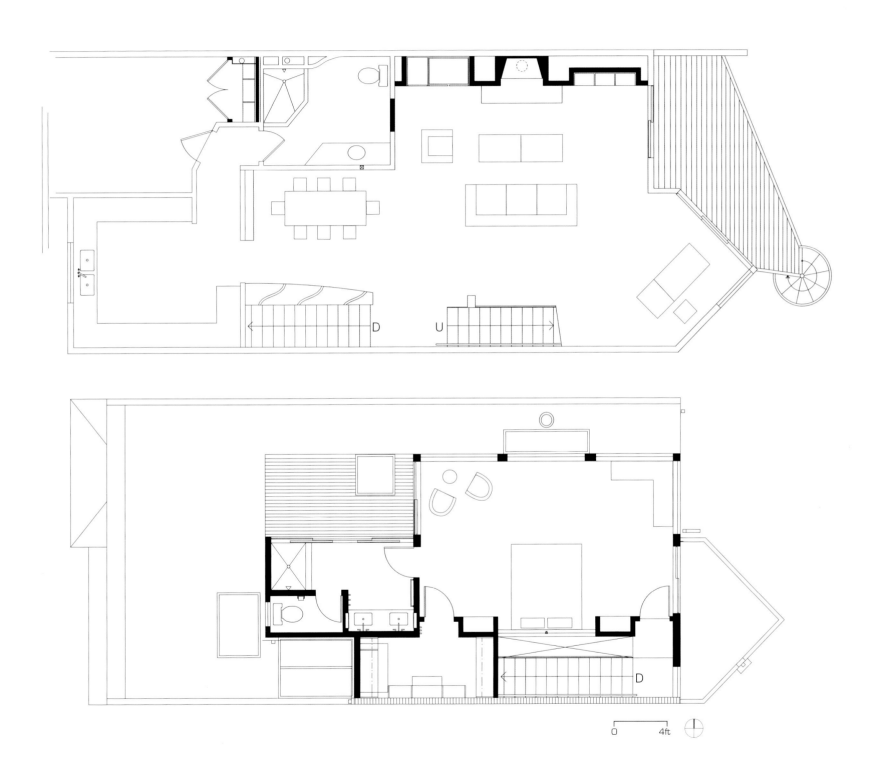

D U

D

0   4ft

Architect: Foster and Partners   Photography: Nigel Young

Architect: RTKL   **Photography:** David Whitcomb

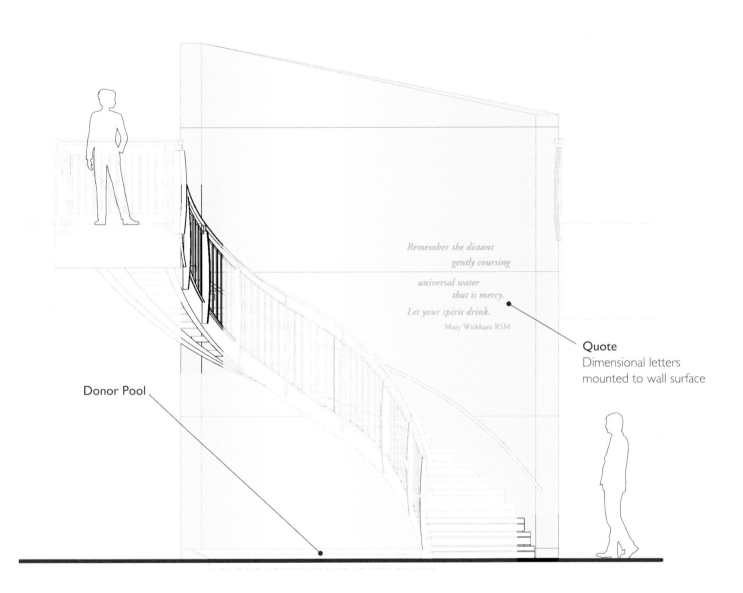

Remember the distant
gently coursing

universal water
that is mercy.

Let your spirit drink.

Mary Wickham RSM

Quote
Dimensional letters
mounted to wall surface

Donor Pool

Architect: Payette   **Photography:** Warren Jagger

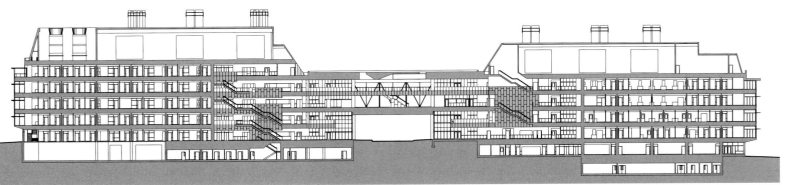

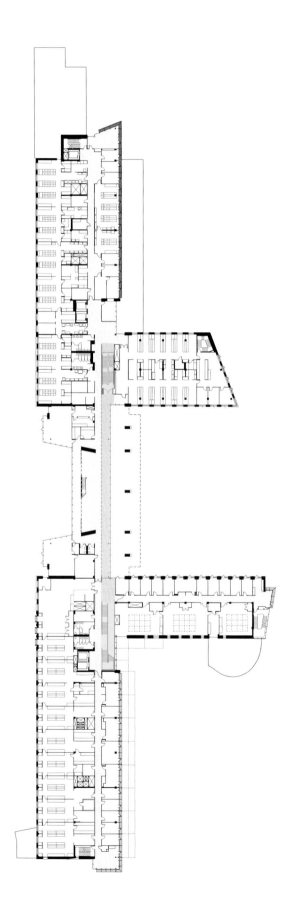

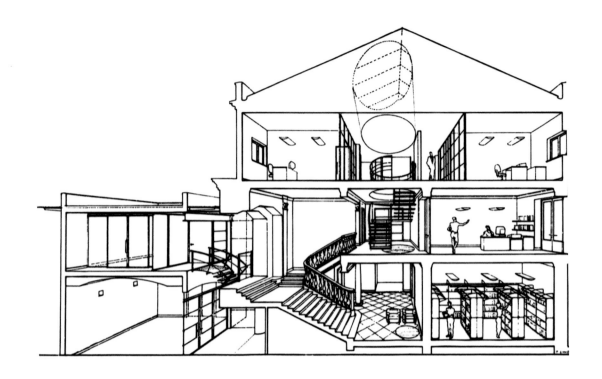

Architect: Jestico + Whiles   Photography: Reto Halme

Architect: Zimmer Gunsul Frasca Partnership   Photography: Timothy Hursley

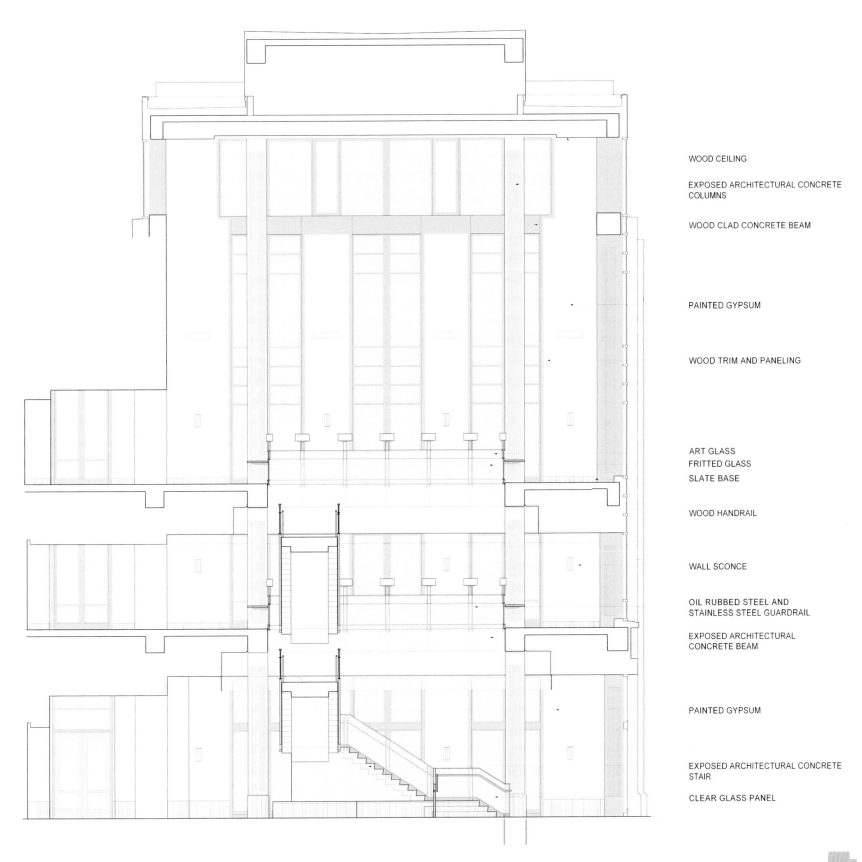

WOOD CEILING

EXPOSED ARCHITECTURAL CONCRETE
COLUMNS

WOOD CLAD CONCRETE BEAM

PAINTED GYPSUM

WOOD TRIM AND PANELING

ART GLASS
FRITTED GLASS
SLATE BASE

WOOD HANDRAIL

WALL SCONCE

OIL RUBBED STEEL AND
STAINLESS STEEL GUARDRAIL

EXPOSED ARCHITECTURAL
CONCRETE BEAM

PAINTED GYPSUM

EXPOSED ARCHITECTURAL CONCRETE
STAIR

CLEAR GLASS PANEL

43

Architect: Platt Byard Dovell White **Photography:** Elliot Kaufman Photography

Architect: Studios Architecture   **Photography:** Tim Griffith

Architect: Foster and Partners   **Photography:** Nigel Young

Architect: 3XNielsen   Photography: Adam Mørk

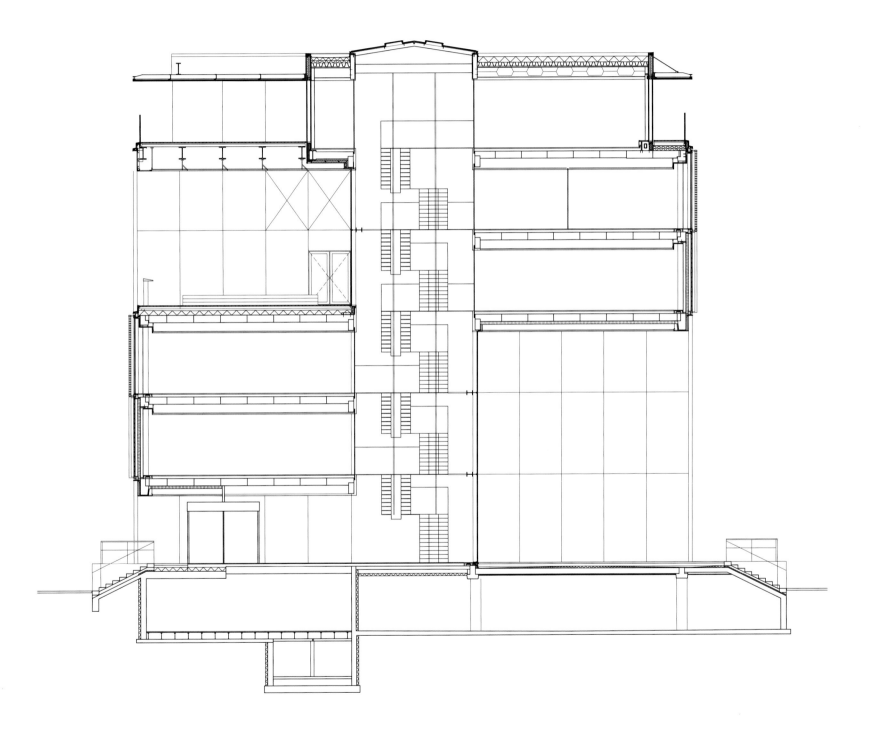

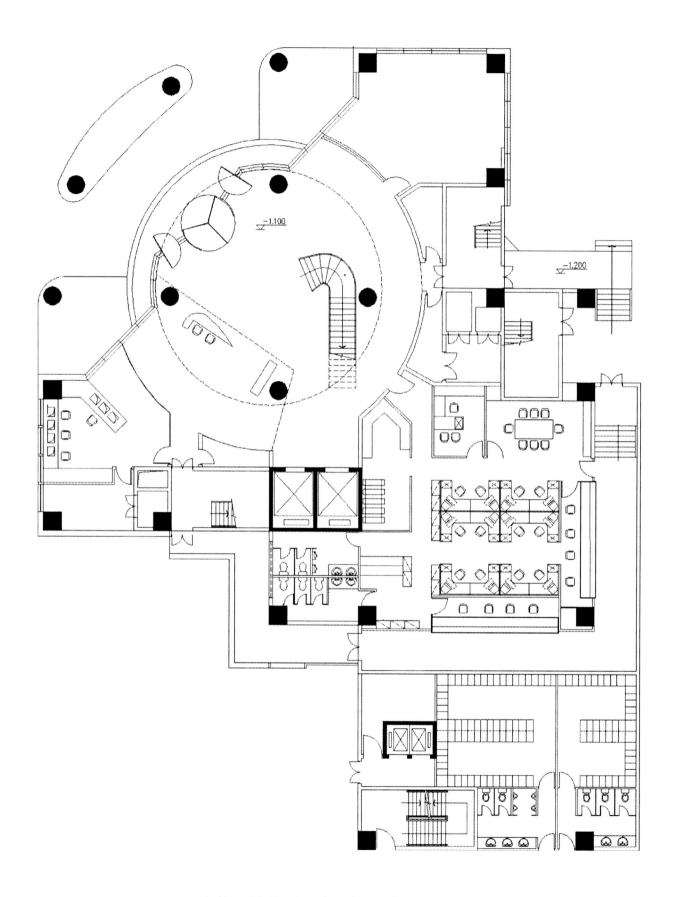

Architect: DPWT Design Ltd.   **Photography**: Mr Diamond Chan

Architect: CCS Architecture   **Photography**: Cesar Rubio

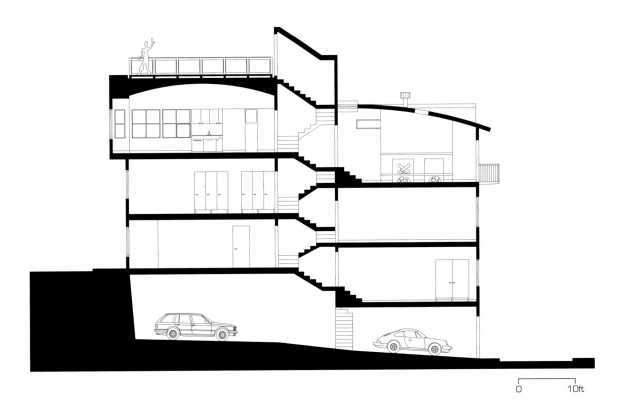

0   10ft

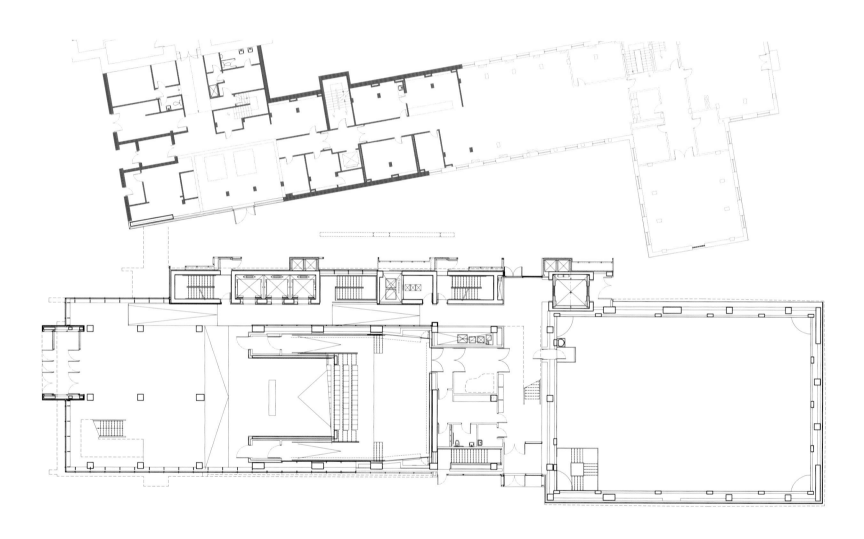

Architect: Saucier + Perrotte Architects   **Photography:** Marc Cramer

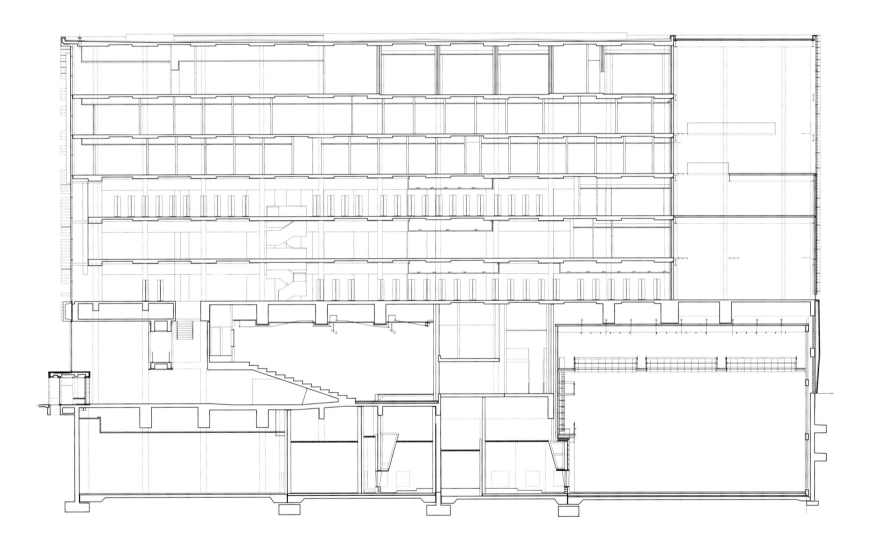

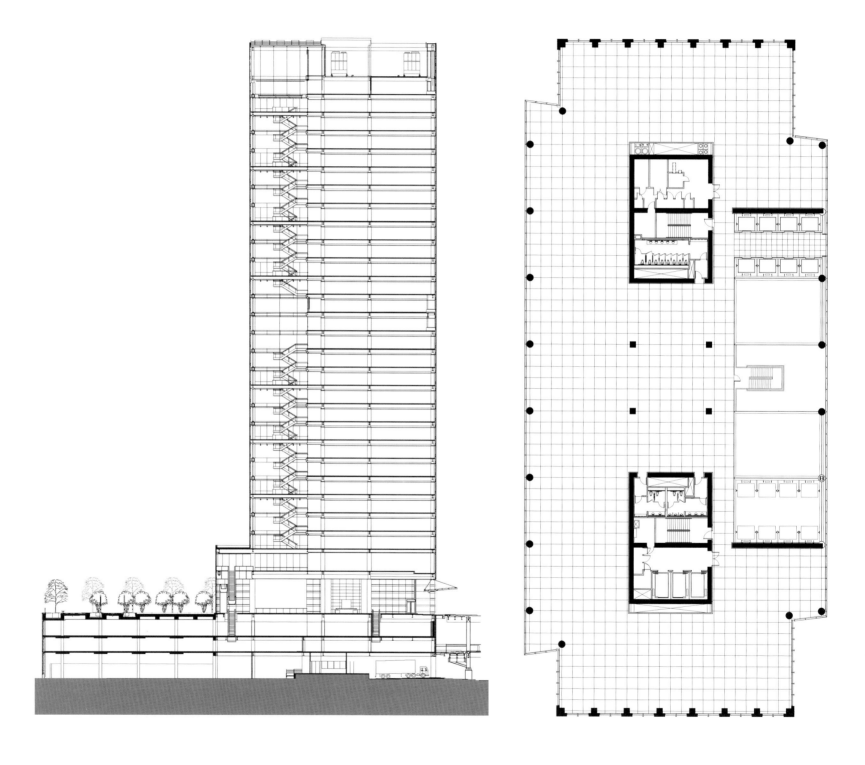

Architect: Goettsch Partners   Photography: Steinkamp/Ballog Photography

Architect: Studios Architecture   Photography: Tim Griffith

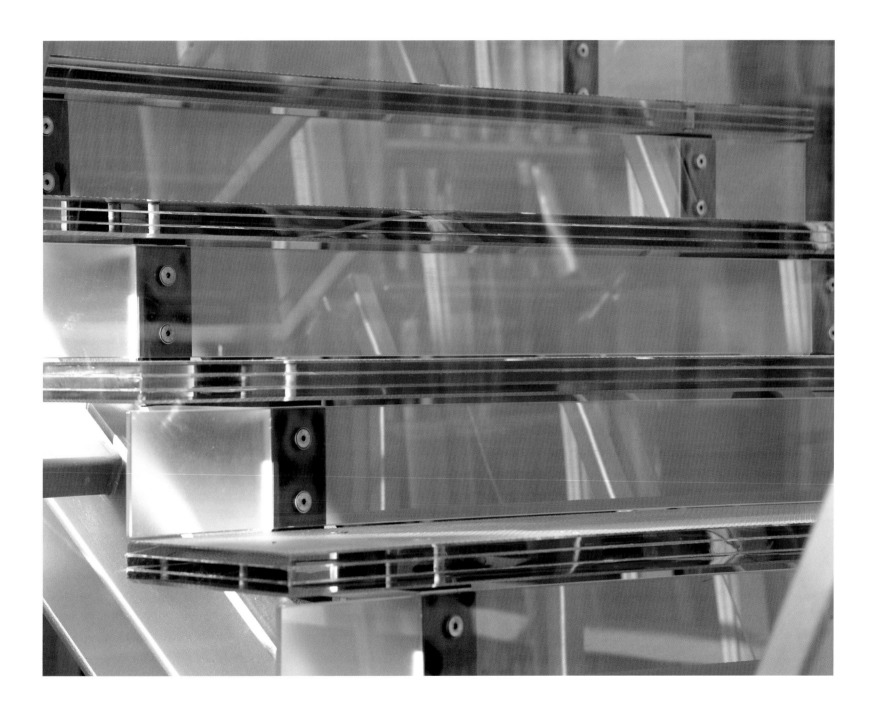

Architect: Payette   Photography: Jeff Goldberg/Esto

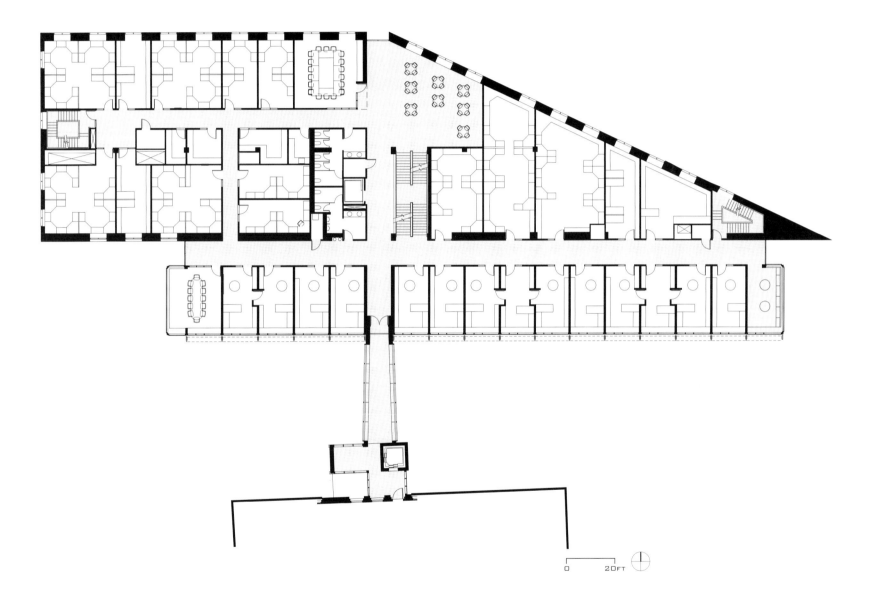

Architect: Helin & Co   Photography: Kari Palsila, Voitto Niemelä

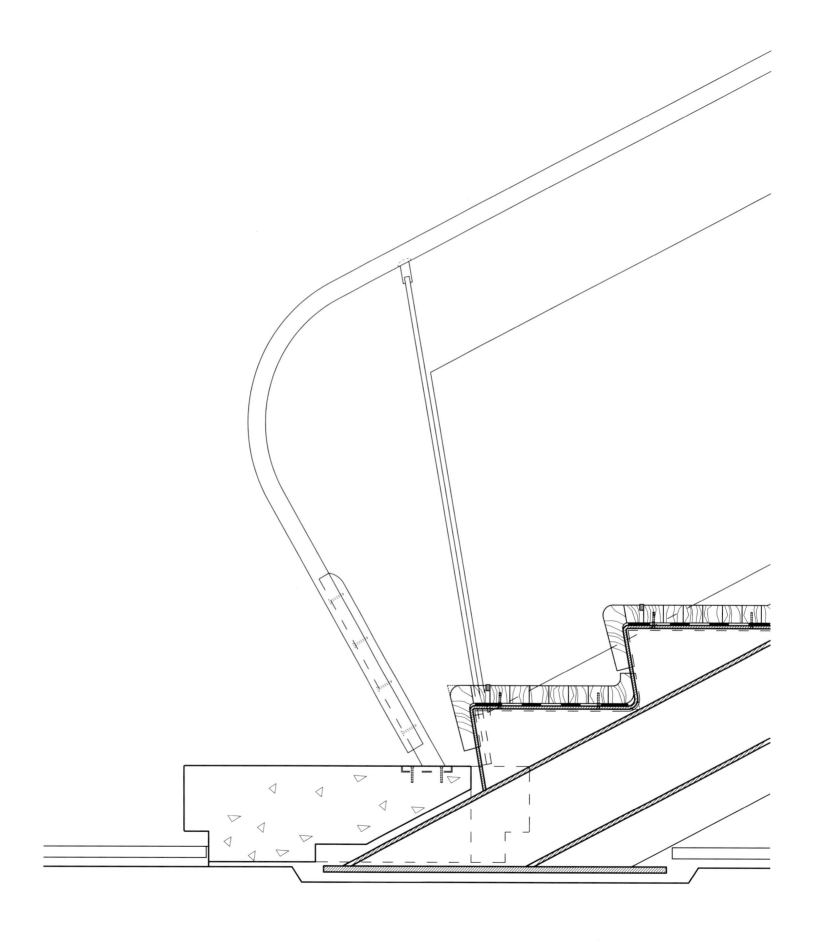

Architect: 3XNielsen   Photography: Adam Mørk

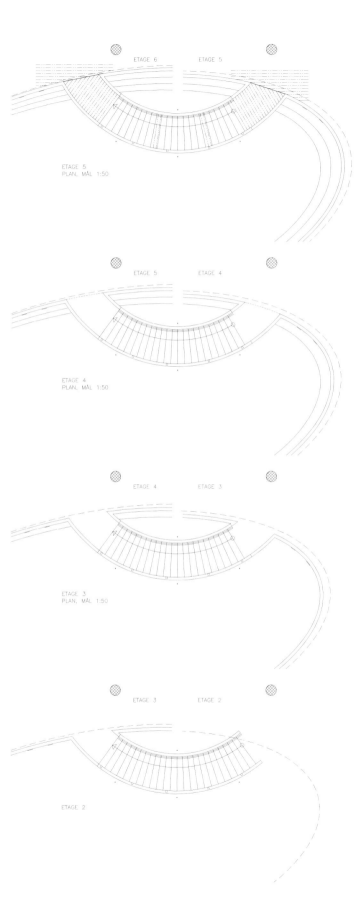

ETAGE 6   ETAGE 5

ETAGE 5
PLAN, MÅL 1:50

ETAGE 5   ETAGE 4

ETAGE 4
PLAN, MÅL 1:50

ETAGE 4   ETAGE 3

ETAGE 3
PLAN, MÅL 1:50

ETAGE 3   ETAGE 2

ETAGE 2

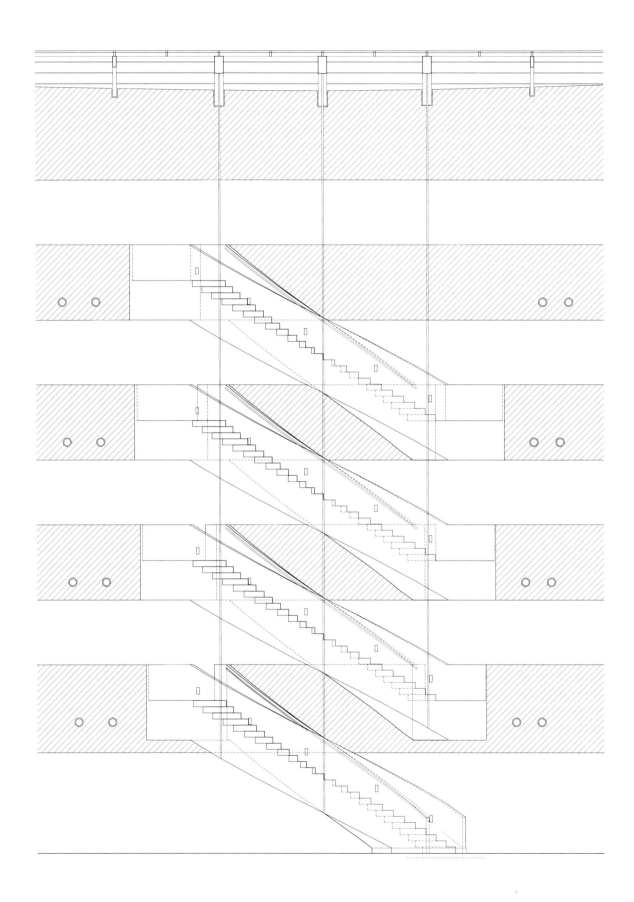

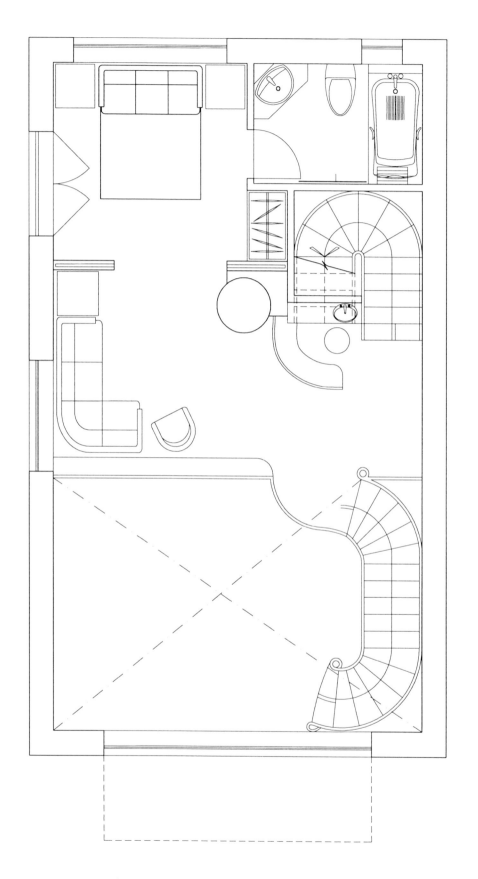

Architect: DPWT Design Ltd.   Photography: Mr Diamond Chan

Architect: Platt Byard Dovell White   **Photography:** Johnathan Wallan

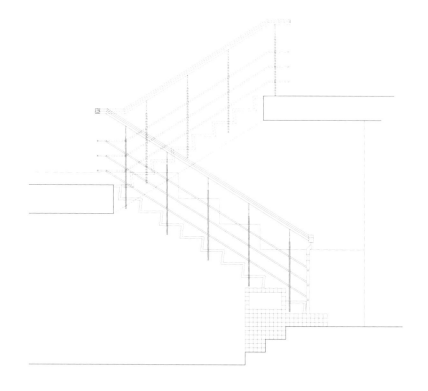

Architect: Damien Murtagh Architects   **Photography:** Gaston Verdicchio

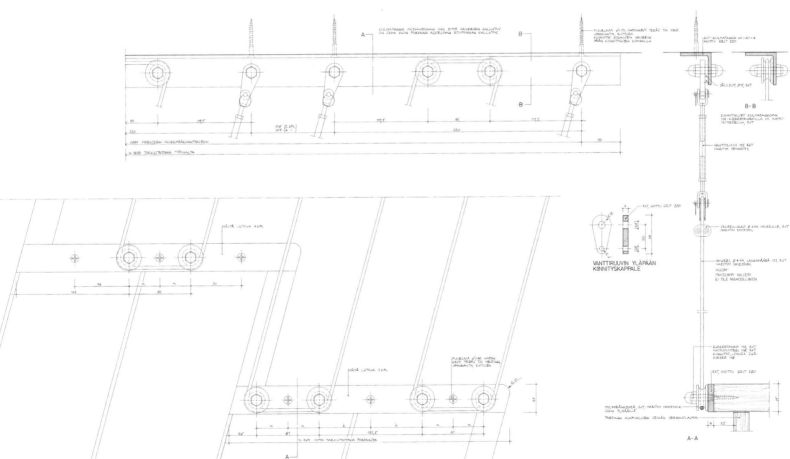

Architect: Helin & Co   Photography: Rauno Traskelin

Architect: Kohn Pedersen Fox Associates   **Photography**: Timothy Hursley

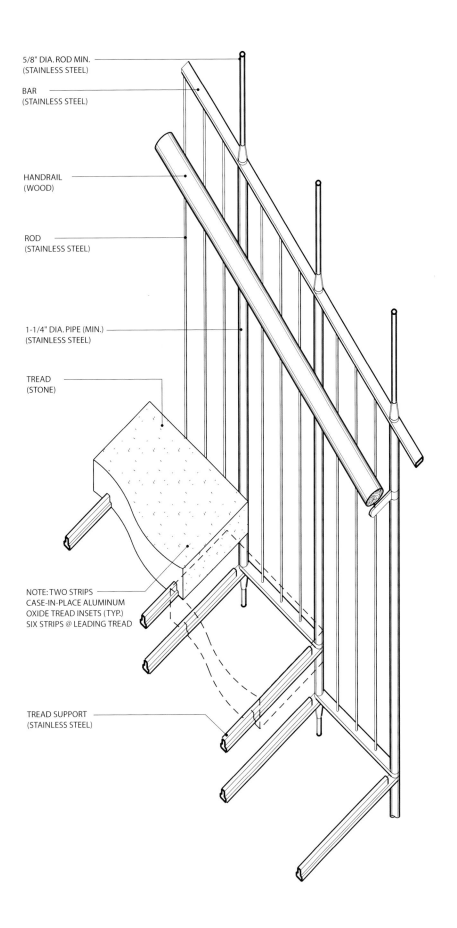

5/8" DIA. ROD MIN.
(STAINLESS STEEL)

BAR
(STAINLESS STEEL)

HANDRAIL
(WOOD)

ROD
(STAINLESS STEEL)

1-1/4" DIA. PIPE (MIN.)
(STAINLESS STEEL)

TREAD
(STONE)

NOTE: TWO STRIPS
CASE-IN-PLACE ALUMINUM
OXIDE TREAD INSETS (TYP.)
SIX STRIPS @ LEADING TREAD

TREAD SUPPORT
(STAINLESS STEEL)

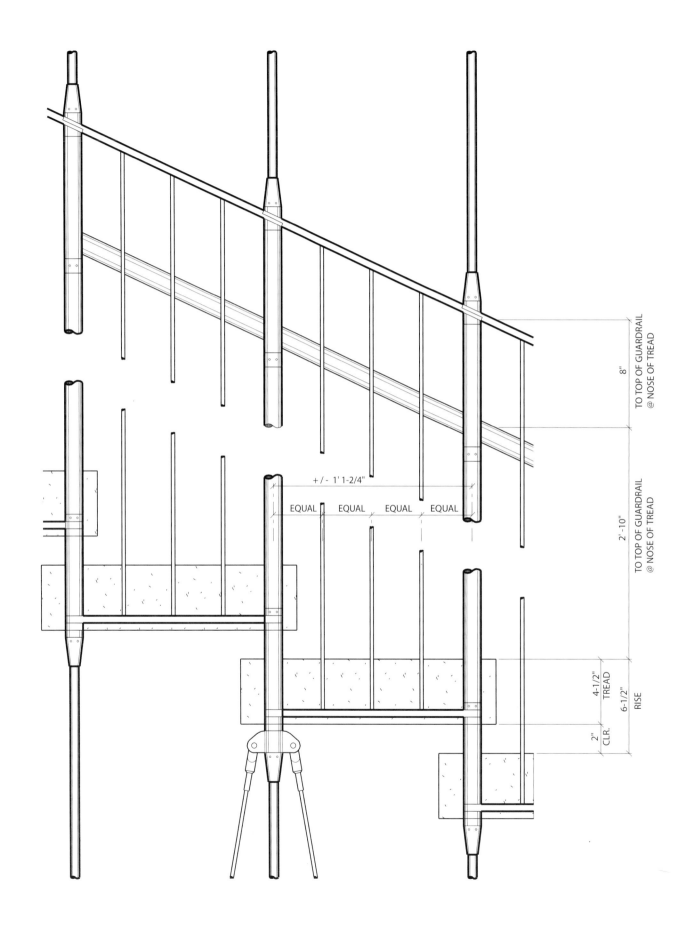

+ / - 1' 1-2/4"

EQUAL   EQUAL   EQUAL   EQUAL

8"

TO TOP OF GUARDRAIL
@ NOSE OF TREAD

2' -10"

TO TOP OF GUARDRAIL
@ NOSE OF TREAD

4-1/2"
TREAD

6-1/2"
RISE

2"
CLR.

84

Architect: Foster and Partners   Photography: Nigel Young

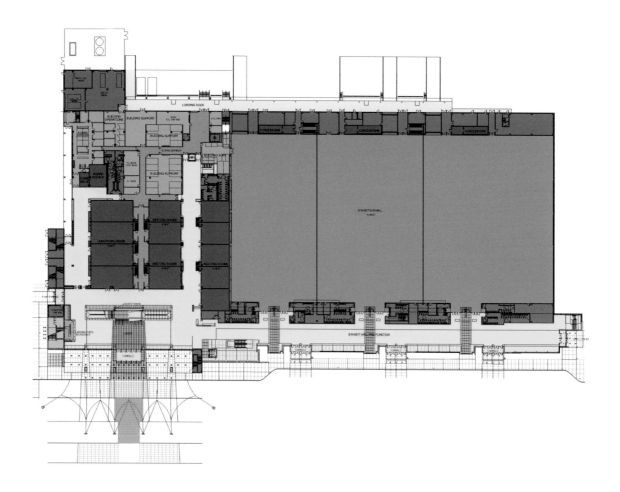

Architect: HOK   Photography: Alan Karchmer, John Lesko

Architect: RTKL   Photography: Erik Kvalsvik

Architect: RTKL   Photography: Feinknopf Photography

Architect: CCS Architecture **Photography:** Tim Griffith

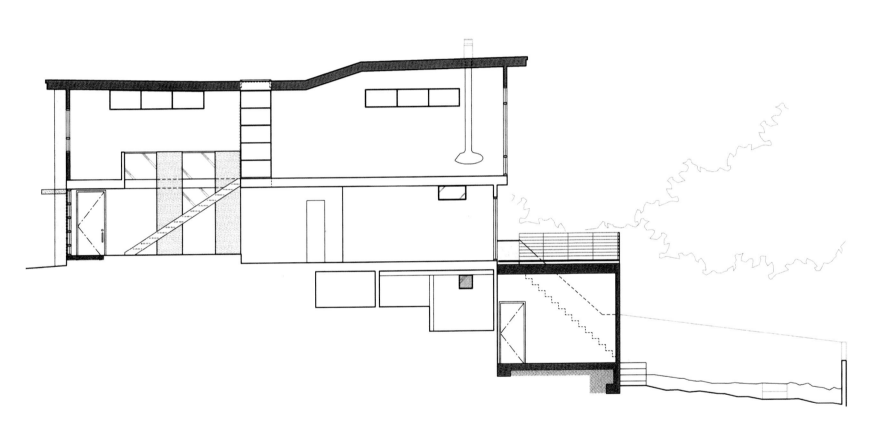

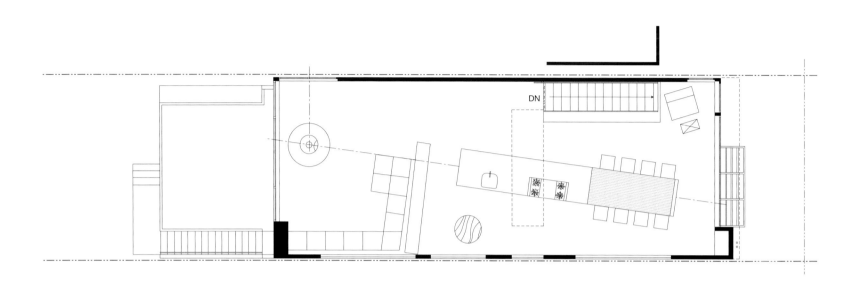

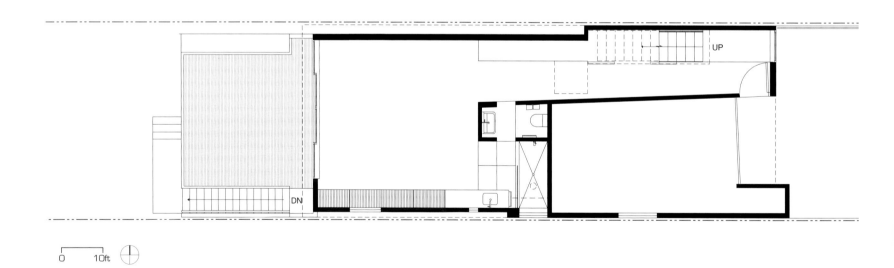

0   10ft

Architect: 3XNielsen   **Photography:** Ivar Mjell

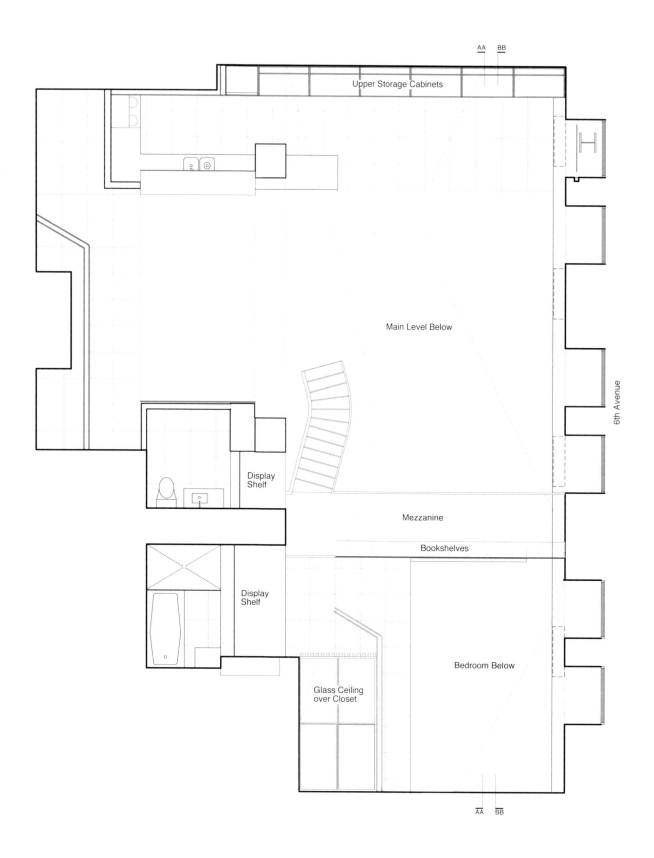

Upper Storage Cabinets

Main Level Below

6th Avenue

Display
Shelf

Mezzanine

Bookshelves

Display
Shelf

Bedroom Below

Glass Ceiling
over Closet

AA BB

AA BB

Architect: Marble Fairbanks   **Photography**: Gregory Goode Photography

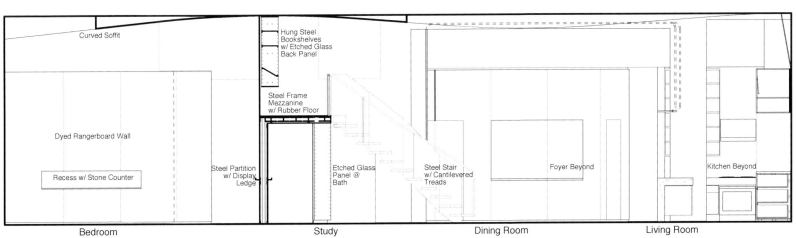

Curved Soffit

Hung Steel
Bookshelves
w/ Etched Glass
Back Panel

Steel Frame
Mezzanine
w/ Rubber Floor

Dyed Rangerboard Wall

Recess w/ Stone Counter

Steel Partition
w/ Display
Ledge

Etched Glass
Panel @
Bath

Steel Stair
w/ Cantilevered
Treads

Foyer Beyond

Kitchen Beyond

Bedroom   Study   Dining Room   Living Room

Architect: Camenzind Evolution   **Photography:** Ferit Kuyas, Camenzind Evolution

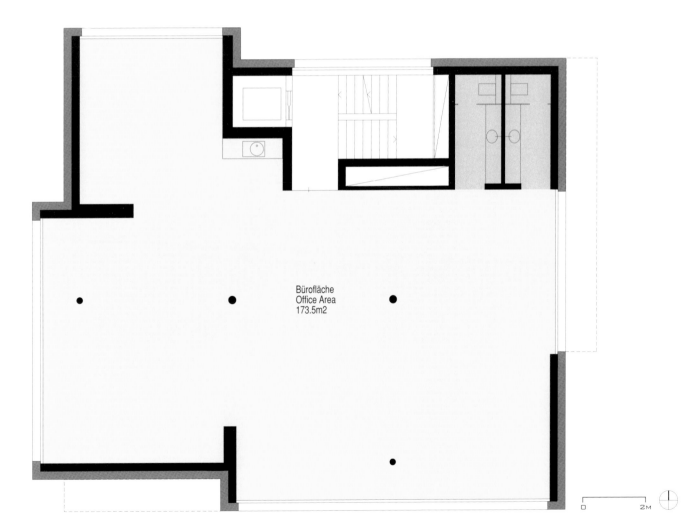

Bürofläche
Office Area
173.5m2

0   2M

Architect: Zimmer Gunsul Frasca Partnership   **Photography:** Eckert and Eckert

Architect: DPWT Design Ltd.   Photography: Mr Diamond Chan

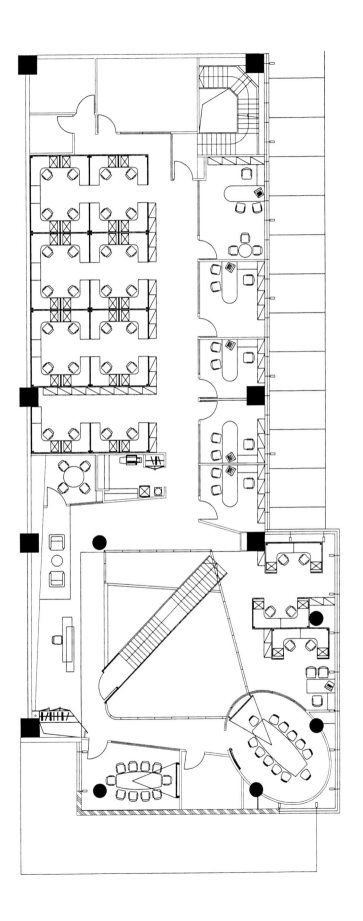

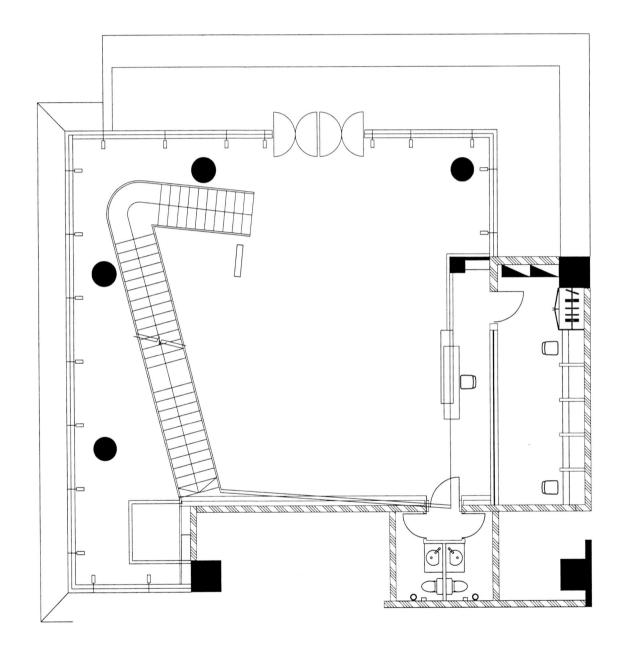

Architect: RTKL   Photography: David Whitcomb

Architect: HOK   Photography: Scott McDonald/Hedrich Blessing

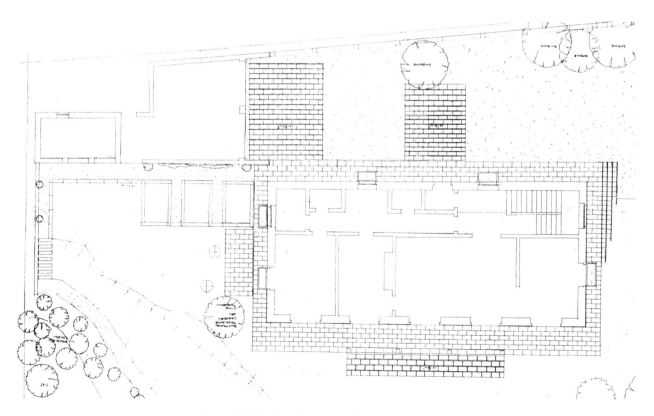

Architect: Hild Und K Architekten   **Photography**: Michael Heinrich

Architect: Hild Und K Architekten   Photography: Michael Heinrich

Architect: Platt Byard Dovell White   Photography: Johnathan Wallan

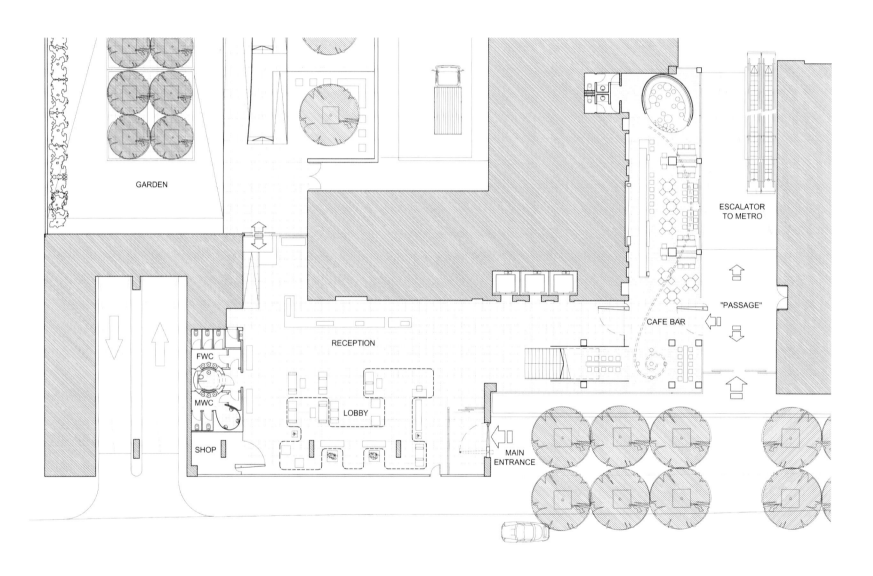

GARDEN

FWC

MWC

SHOP

RECEPTION

LOBBY

MAIN
ENTRANCE

CAFE BAR

"PASSAGE"

ESCALATOR
TO METRO

Architect: Jestico + Whiles   **Photography**: Ales Jungmann

Architect: HLW   Photography: Benny Chan, Fotoworks

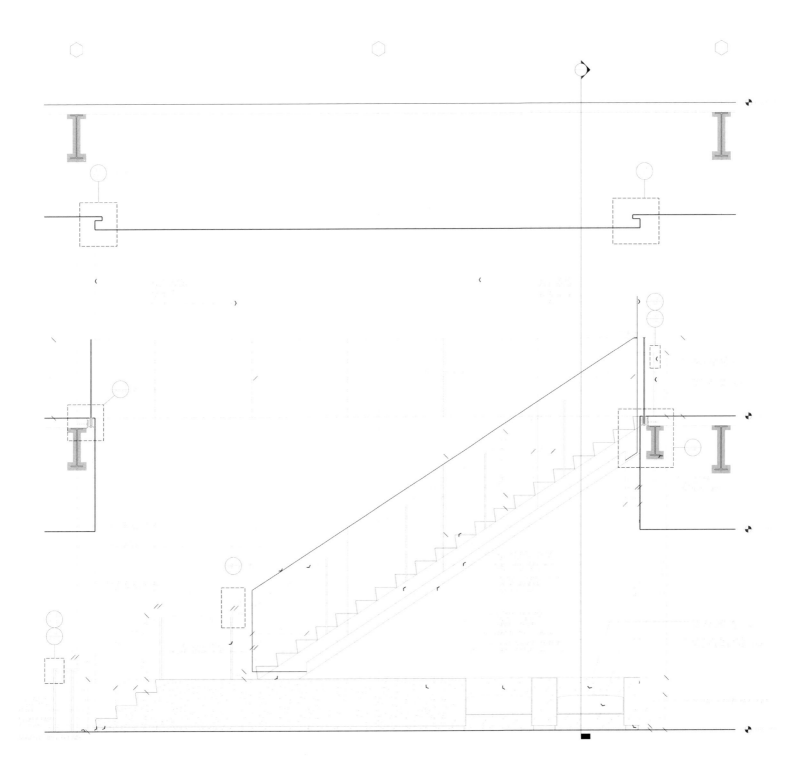

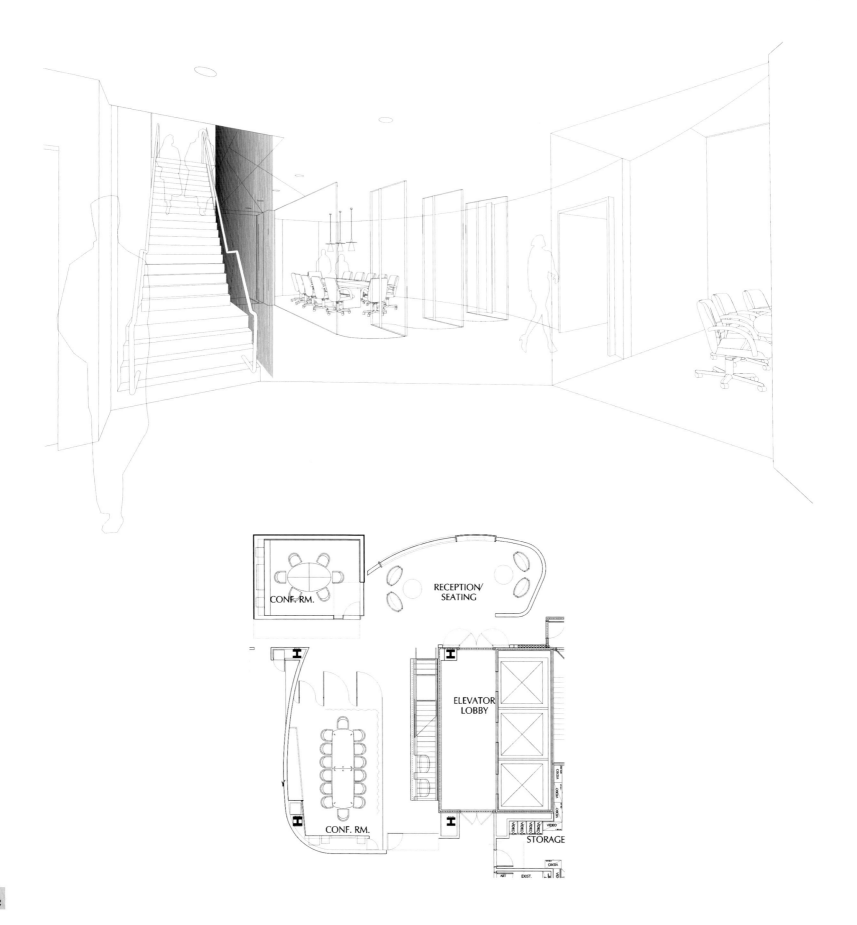

CONF. RM.

RECEPTION/
SEATING

ELEVATOR
LOBBY

CONF. RM.

STORAGE

VIDEO

ART   EXIST.

Architect: Studios Architecture   **Photography**: Luc Boegly

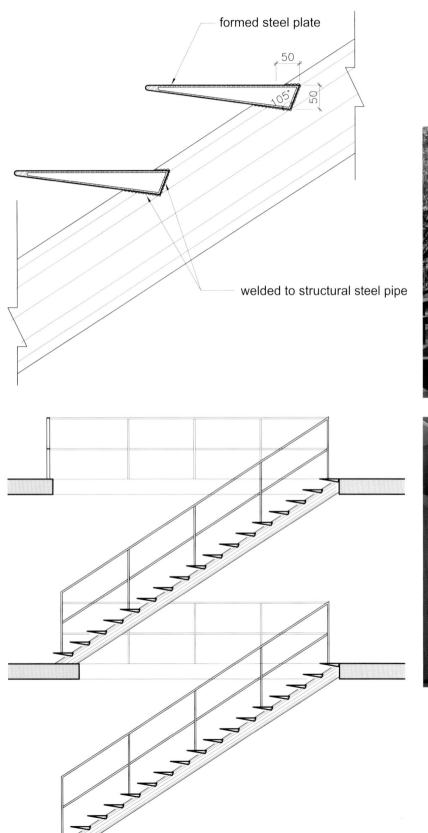

formed steel plate

50

105°

50

welded to structural steel pipe

Architect: J J Pan & Partners   Photography: J J Pan & Partners, Jeffrey Cheng

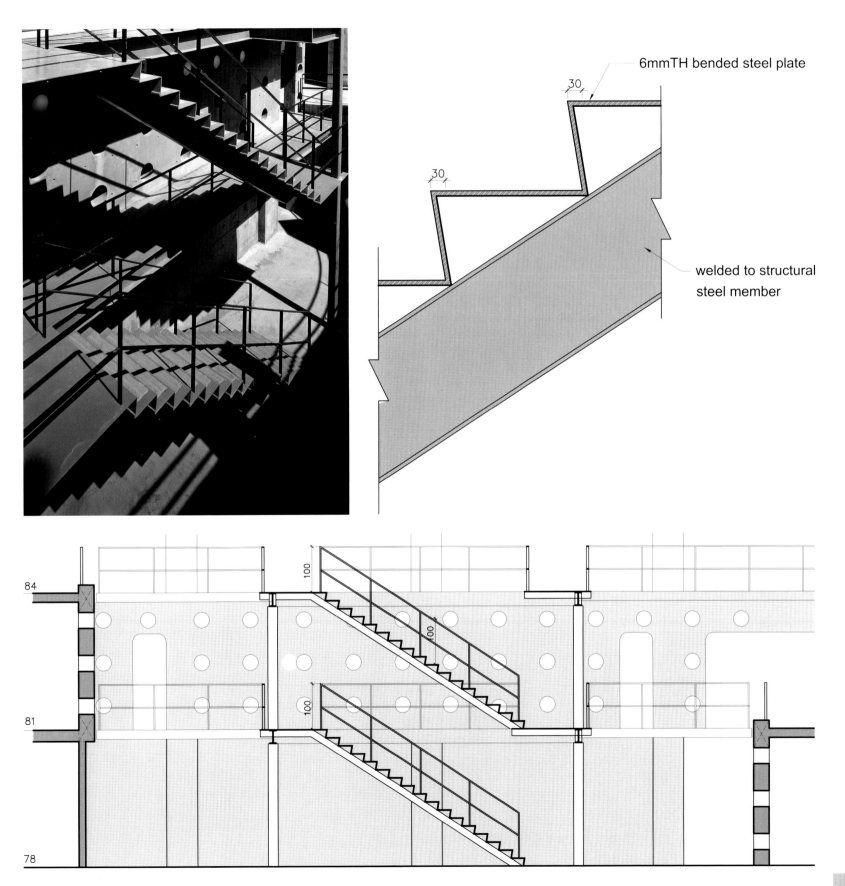

6mmTH bended steel plate

30

30

welded to structural
steel member

84

81

78

100

100

100

127

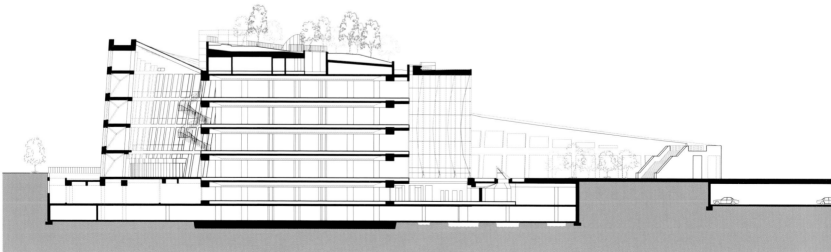

Architect: Moshe Safdie   **Photography:** Timothy Hursley

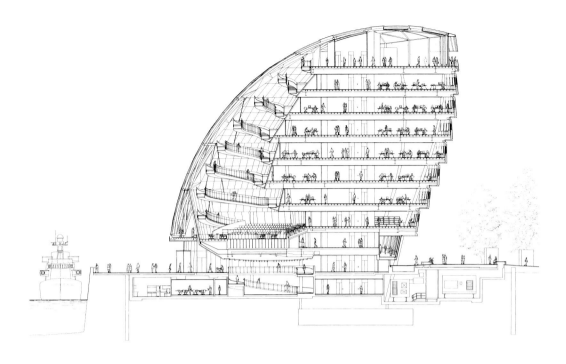

Architect: Foster and Partners   **Photography:** Nigel Young

Architect: Saucier + Perrotte Architects   **Photography:** Marc Cramer

Architect: Coy & Yointis   **Photography:** Peter Clarke

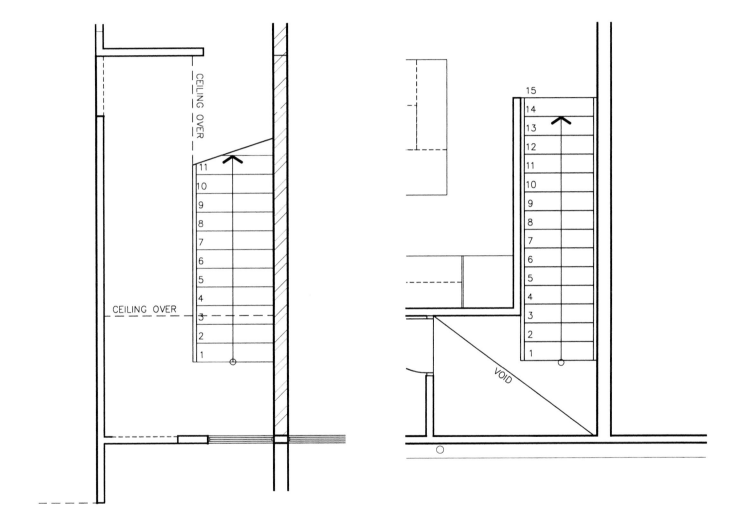

CEILING OVER

CEILING OVER

11
10
9
8
7
6
5
4
3
2
1

15
14
13
12
11
10
9
8
7
6
5
4
3
2
1

VOID

Architect: RTKL   **Photography:** David Whitcomb

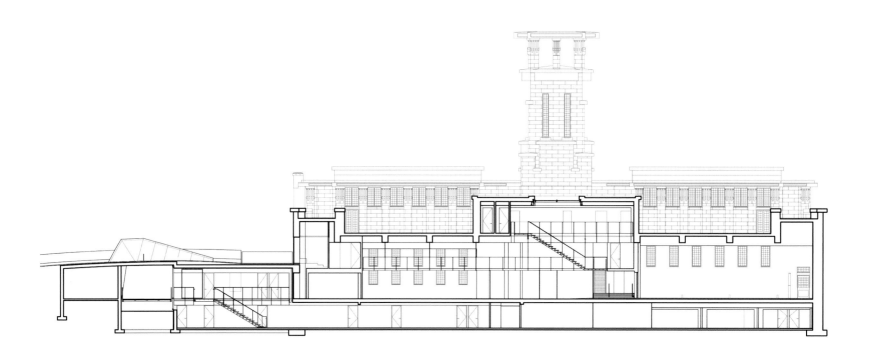

Architect: Saucier + Perrotte Architects   **Photography:** Marc Cramer

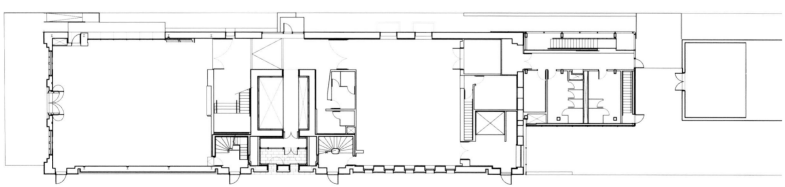

Architect: HLW   Photography: Mr Zhonghai Shen

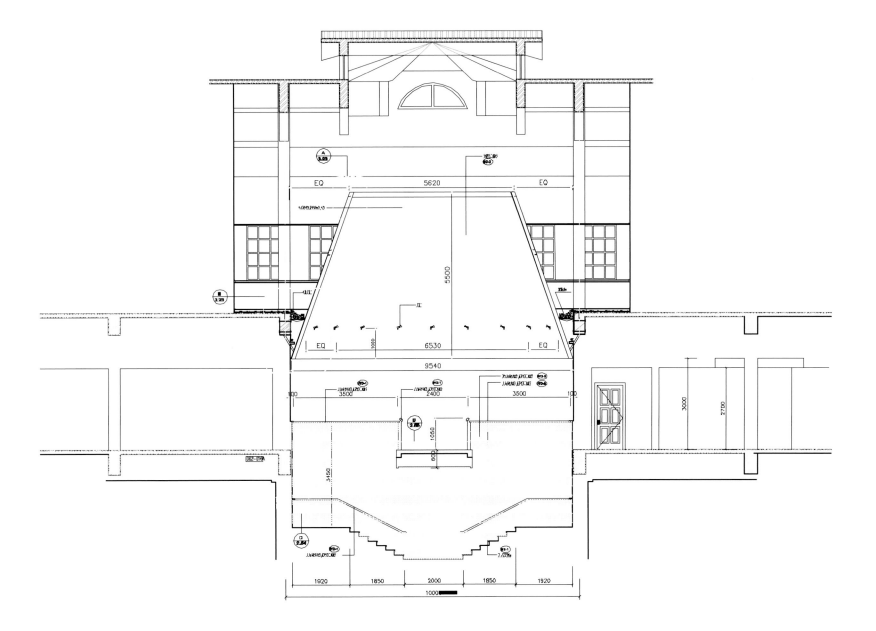

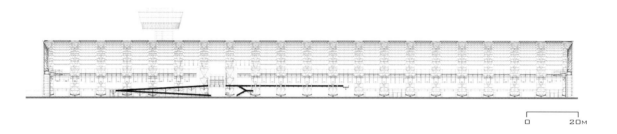

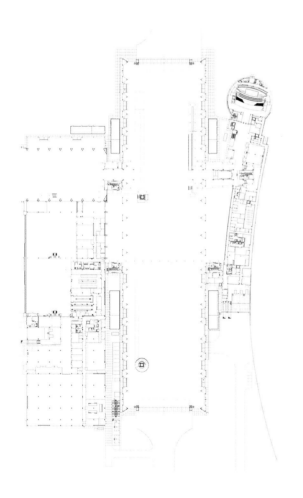

Architect: HOK   Photography: Joseph Romeo, Elizabeth Gil Lui

Architect: DPWT Design Ltd.   Photography: Mr Diamond Chan

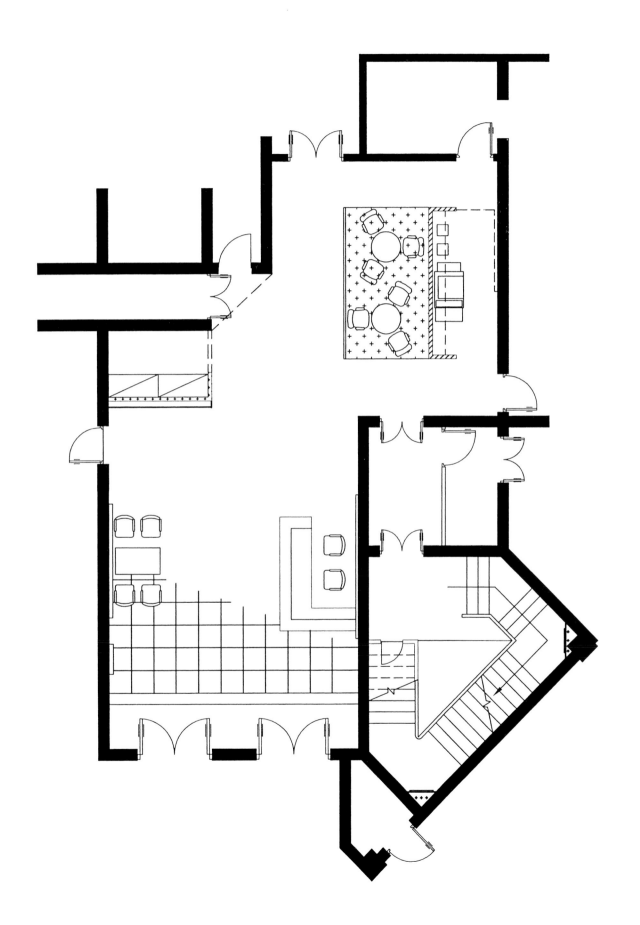

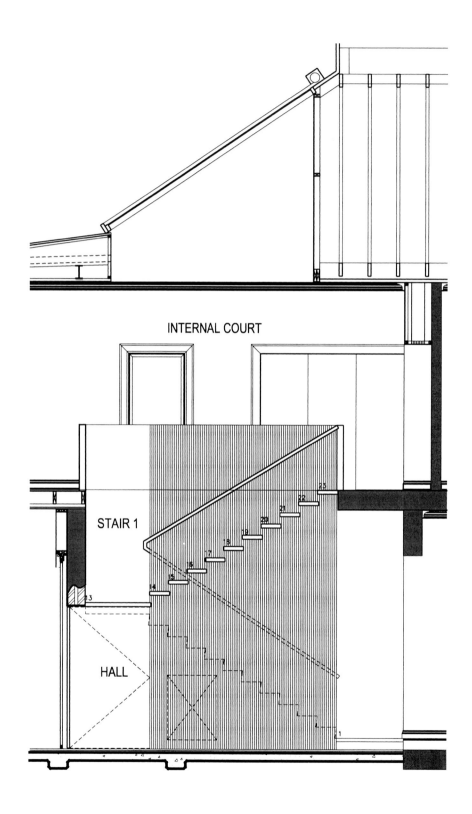

INTERNAL COURT

STAIR 1

13

HALL

Architect: Coy & Yointis   **Photography**: Peter Clarke

Architect: Bromley Caldari Architects   **Photography:** Eric Laignel

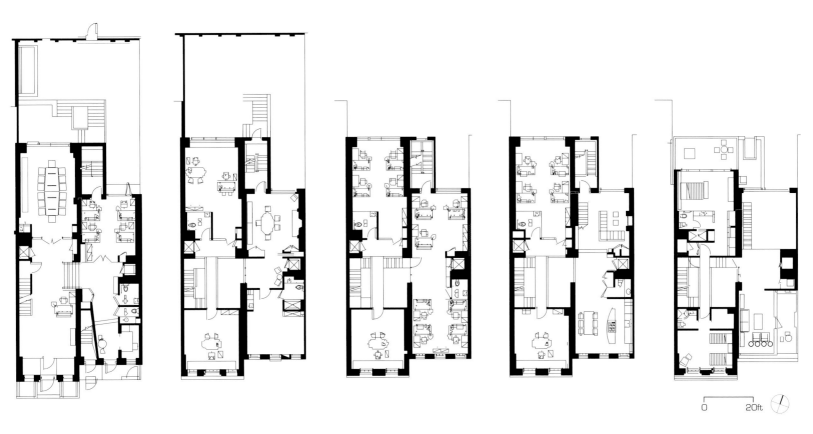

153

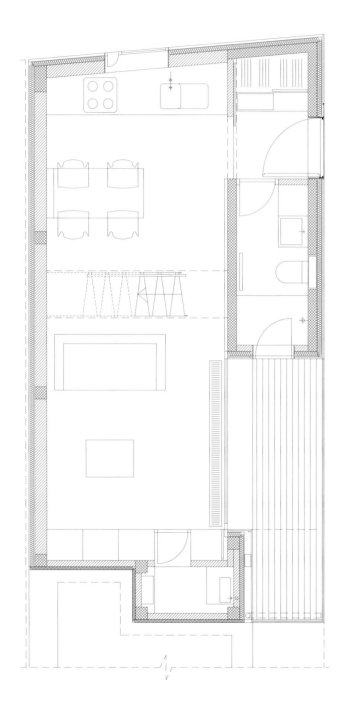

Architect: Dekleva Gregoric arhitekti   Photography: Matevz Paternoster

Architect: Helin & Co   Photography: Voitto Niemelä

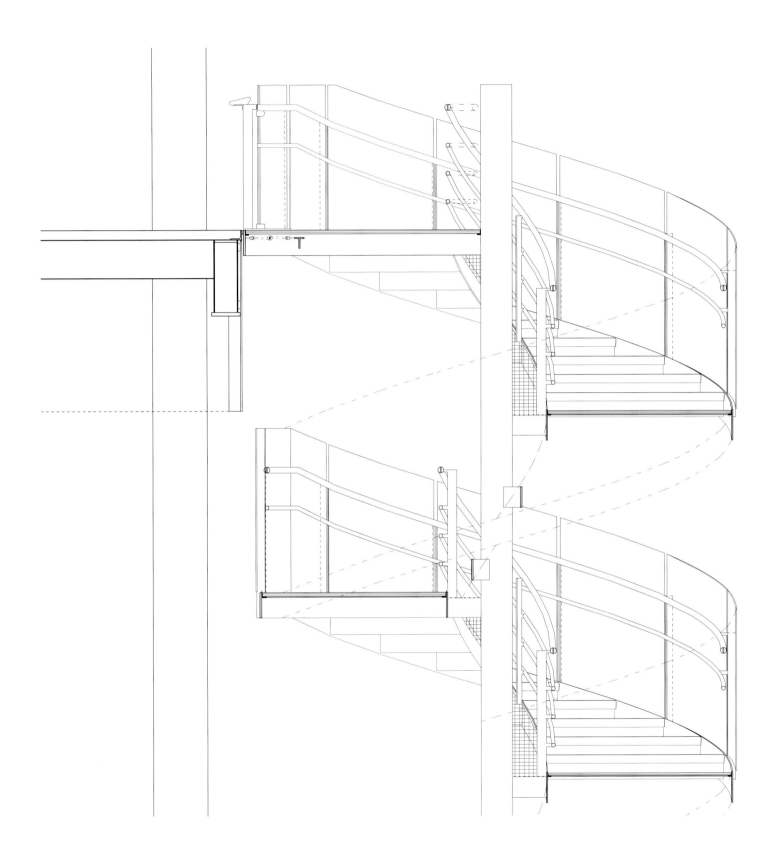

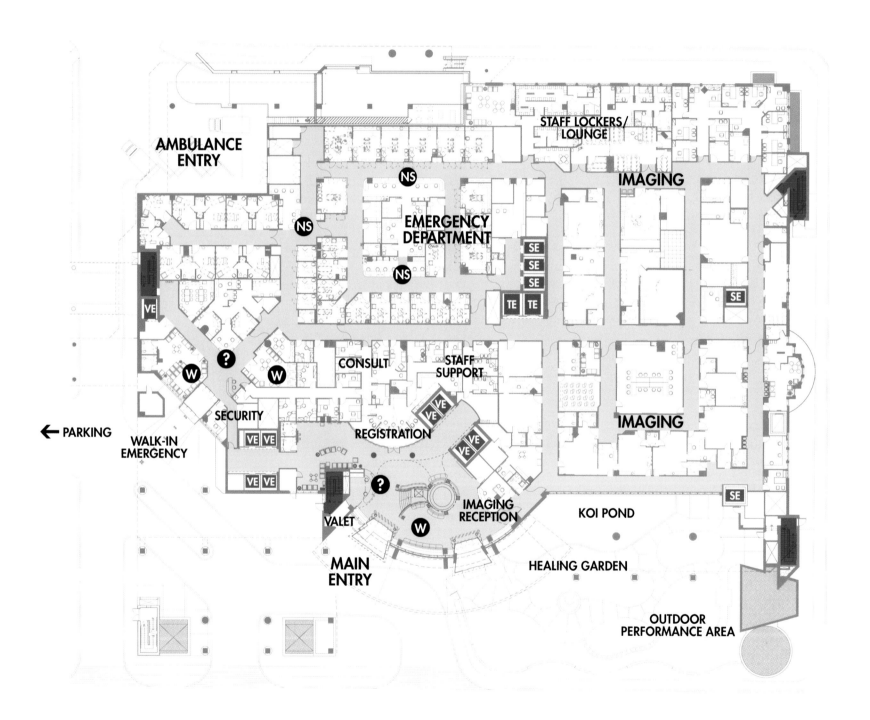

AMBULANCE ENTRY

STAFF LOCKERS/ LOUNGE

IMAGING

NS

NS

EMERGENCY DEPARTMENT

SE
SE
SE

TE TE

NS

SE

CONSULT

STAFF SUPPORT

W

W

IMAGING

SE

← PARKING

SECURITY

VE VE

REGISTRATION

VE
VE

VE
VE

WALK-IN EMERGENCY

VE VE

IMAGING RECEPTION

KOI POND

VALET

W

MAIN ENTRY

HEALING GARDEN

SE

OUTDOOR PERFORMANCE AREA

Architect: Earl Swensson Associates, Inc.   **Photography:** Craig Dugan/Hedrich Blessing

Architect: RTKL   Photography: Tim Griffith

Architect: Jestico + Whiles   Photography: James Morris

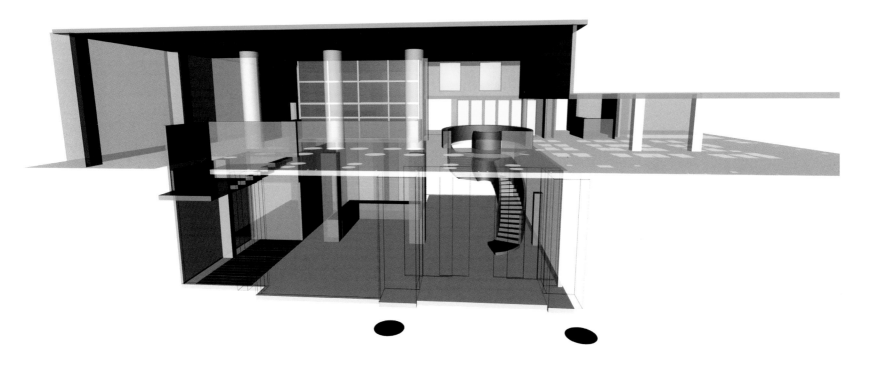

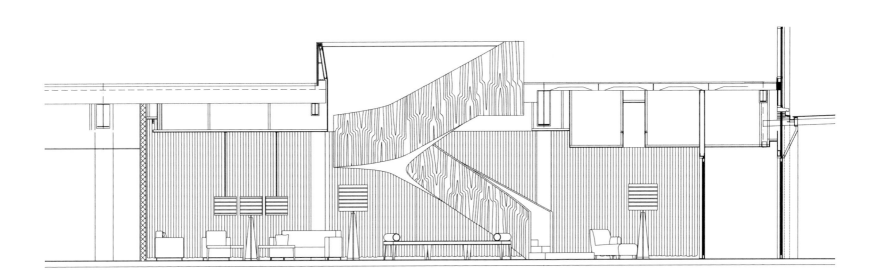

Architect: Parker Durrant International   **Photography:** Farshid Assassi

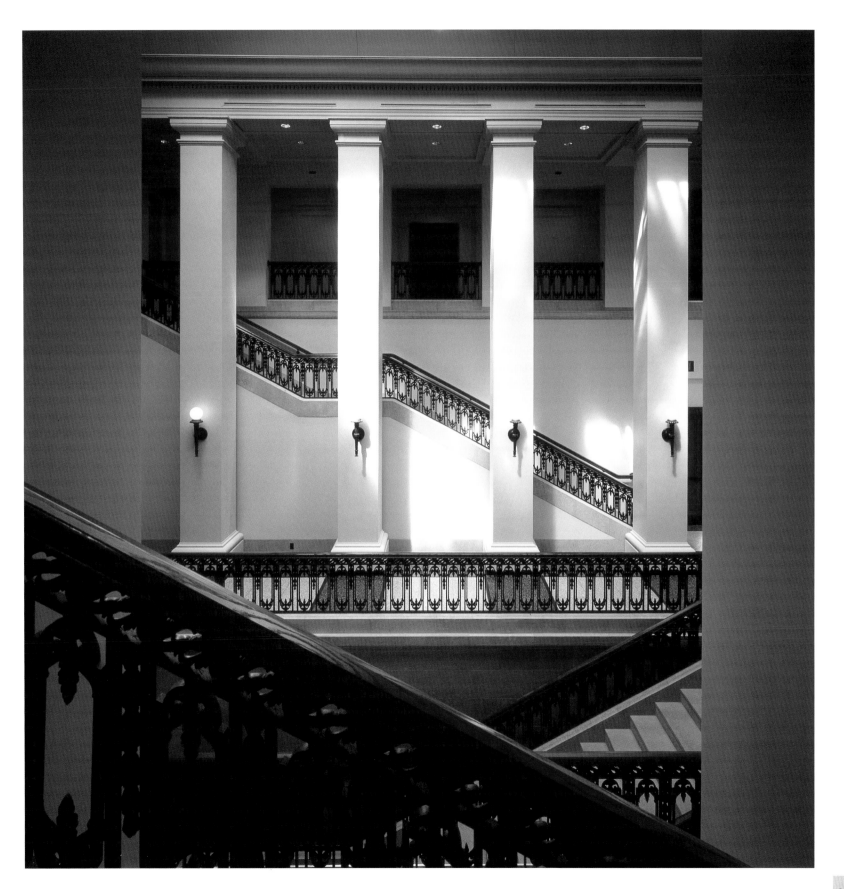

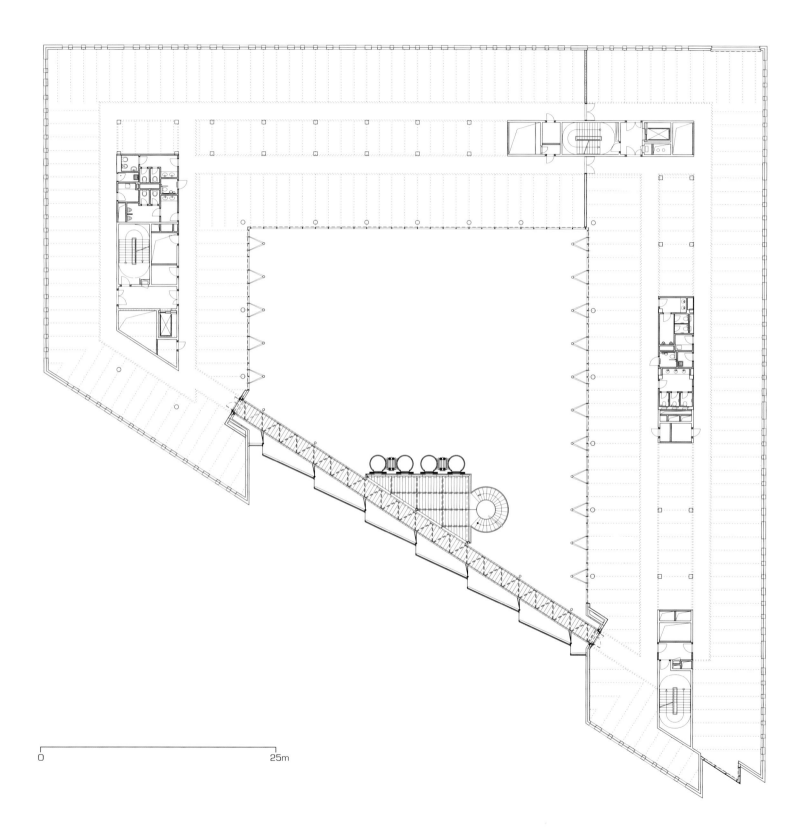

Architect: Kohn Pedersen Fox Associates   Photography: H.G. Esch

0   25m

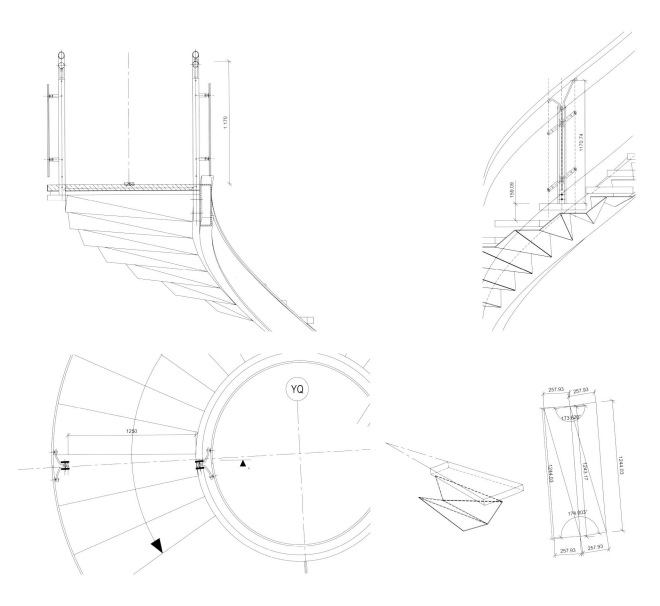

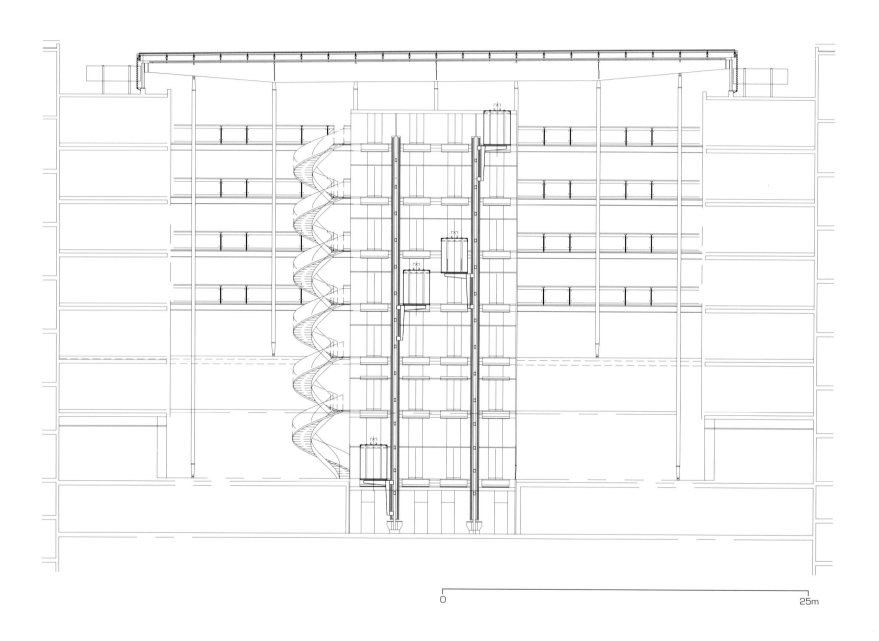

0 25m

Architect: Jestico + Whiles   Photography: Peter Cook

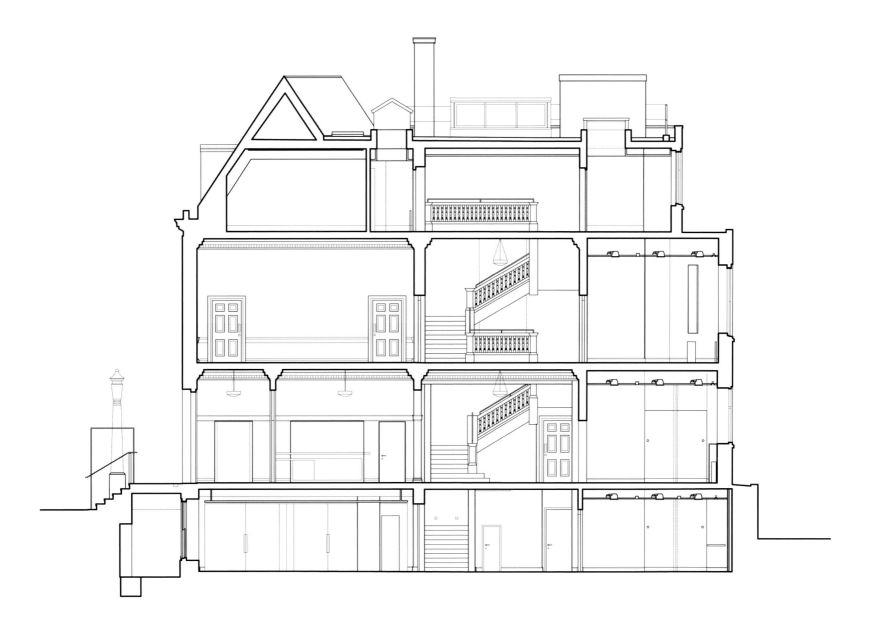

Architect: HOK   Photography: Jim Maguire

Architect: AMA Architects (Pty) Ltd   **Photography**: Lana Myburgh

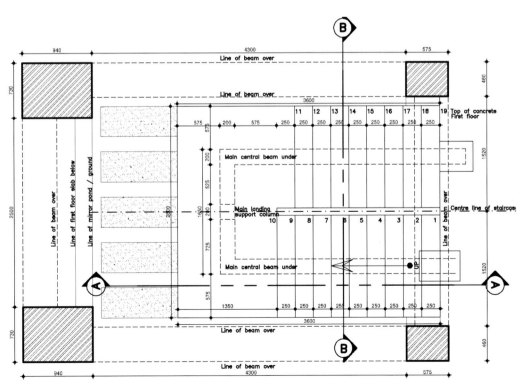

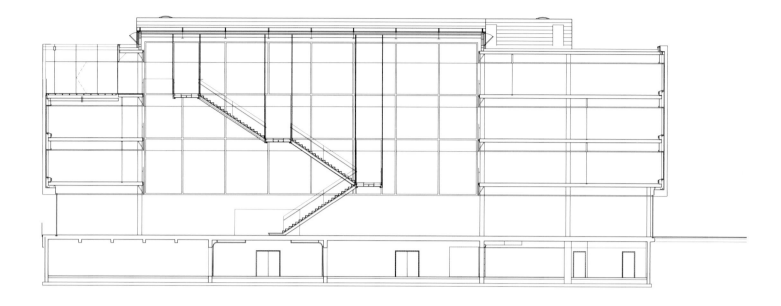

Architect: 3XNielsen   Photography: Adam Mørk

Architect: RTKL   **Photography:** David Whitcomb

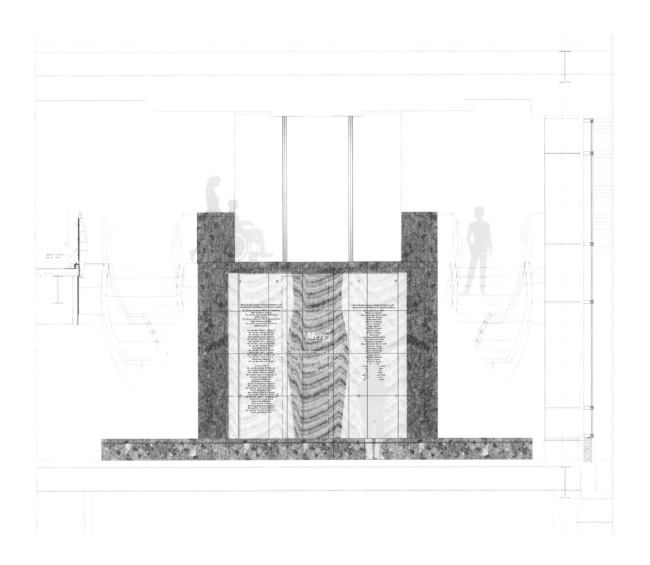

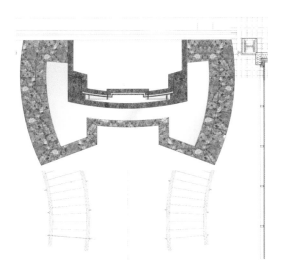

Architect: Studios Architecture   Photography: Luc Boegly

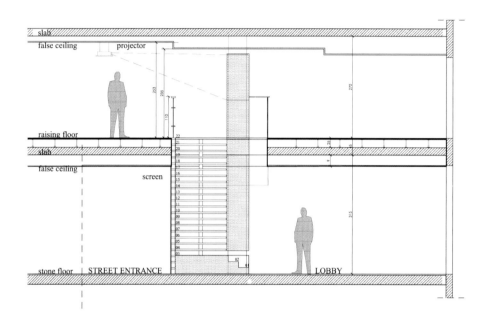

slab
false ceiling · projector
raising floor
slab
false ceiling · screen
stone floor · STREET ENTRANCE · LOBBY

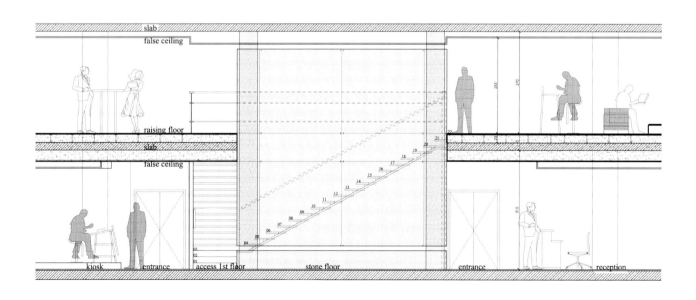

slab
false ceiling
raising floor
slab
false ceiling
kiosk · entrance · access 1st floor · stone floor · entrance · reception

Architect: Baneke, Van Der Hoeven   **Photography:** Ton de Bruin

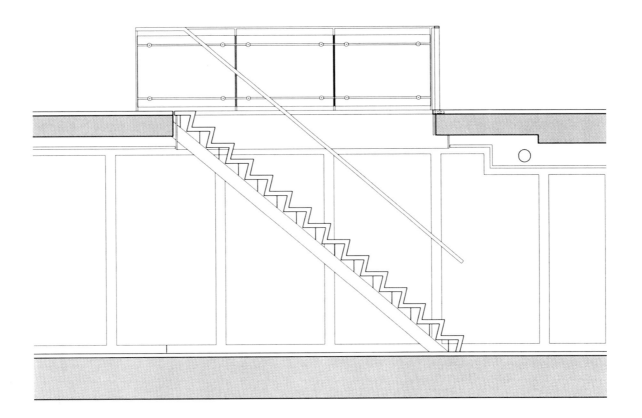

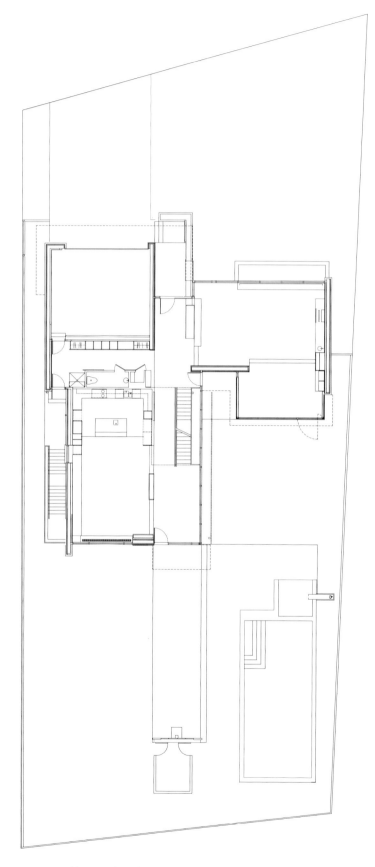

Architect: 3rd Uncle Design   Photography: Andrej Kopac

Architect: Foster and Partners   **Photography:** Nigel Young

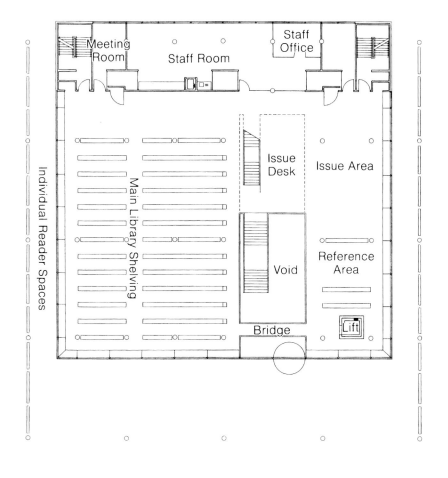

Meeting Room

Staff Room

Staff Office

Individual Reader Spaces

Main Library Shelving

Issue Desk

Issue Area

Void

Reference Area

Bridge

Lift

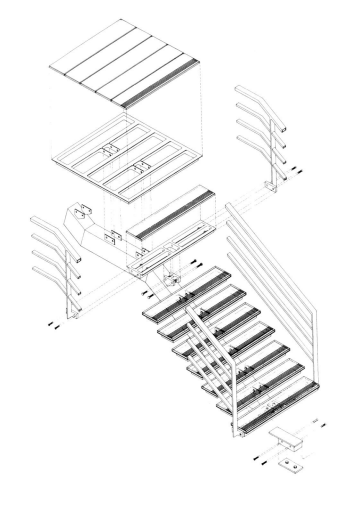

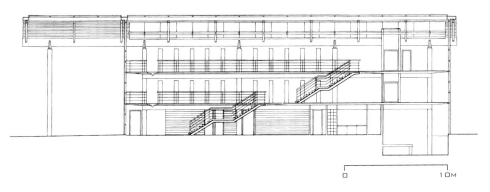

0   10м

Architect: Damien Murtagh Architects   **Photography:** Gaston Verdicchio

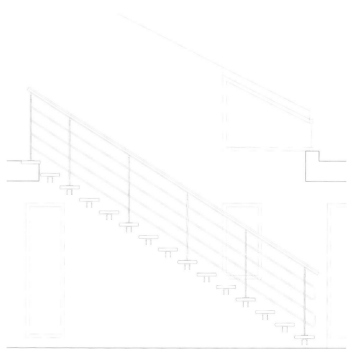

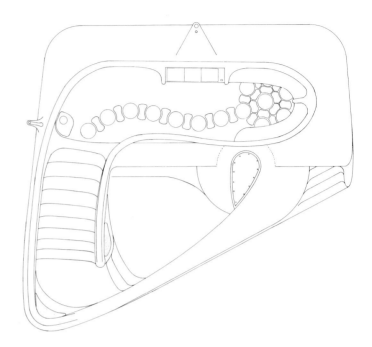

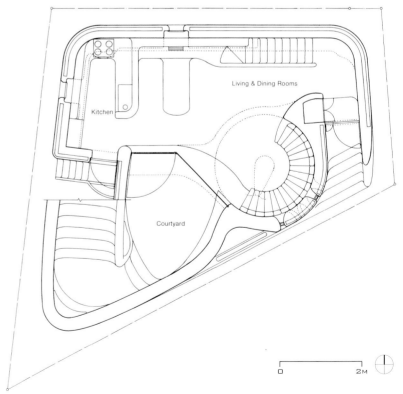

Living & Dining Rooms

Kitchen

Courtyard

0 2M

Architect: Ushida Findlay Partnership Co., Ltd. **Photography:** Tim Giffith

Architect: Saucier + Perrotte Architects   Photography: Marc Cramer

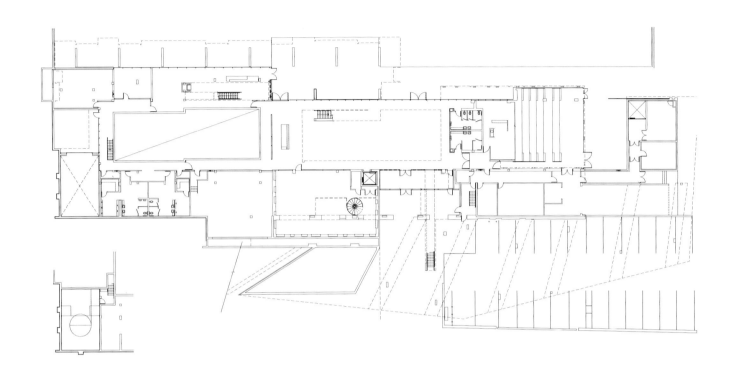

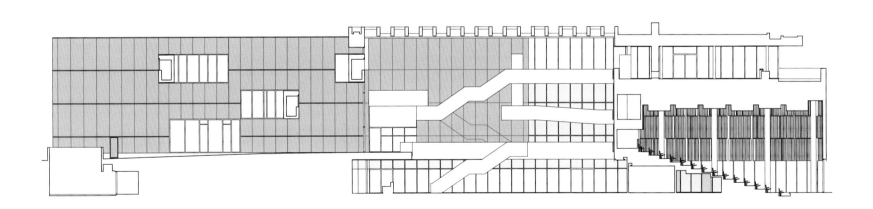

Architect: Payette   Photography: Warren Jagger

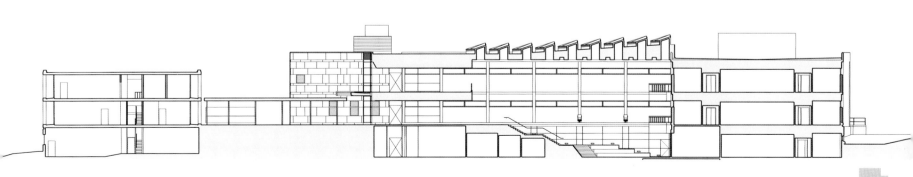

Architect: CCS Architecture   **Photography:** Eric Laignel

Architect: HOK   Photography: Rob Solomon

Architect: Powers Brown   Photography: Dror Baldinger

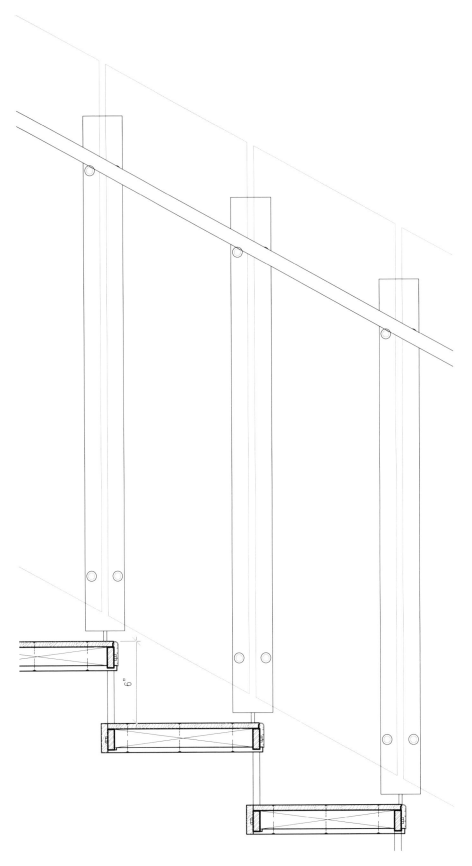

6"

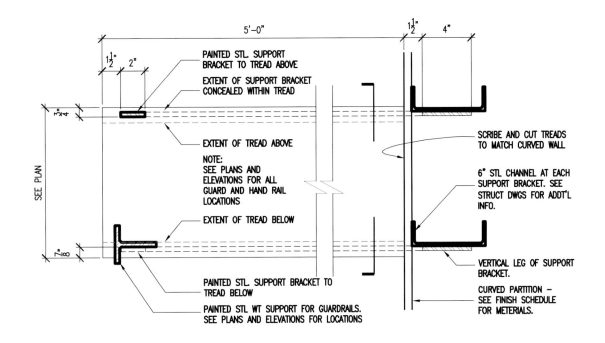

5'-0"

1½" 4"

1½" 2"

3¾"

PAINTED STL. SUPPORT
BRACKET TO TREAD ABOVE

EXTENT OF SUPPORT BRACKET
CONCEALED WITHIN TREAD

SEE PLAN

EXTENT OF TREAD ABOVE

NOTE:
SEE PLANS AND
ELEVATIONS FOR ALL
GUARD AND HAND RAIL
LOCATIONS

EXTENT OF TREAD BELOW

7⅛"

PAINTED STL. SUPPORT BRACKET TO
TREAD BELOW

PAINTED STL WT SUPPORT FOR GUARDRAILS.
SEE PLANS AND ELEVATIONS FOR LOCATIONS

SCRIBE AND CUT TREADS
TO MATCH CURVED WALL

6" STL CHANNEL AT EACH
SUPPORT BRACKET. SEE
STRUCT DWGS FOR ADDT'L
INFO.

VERTICAL LEG OF SUPPORT
BRACKET.

CURVED PARTITION –
SEE FINISH SCHEDULE
FOR METERIALS.

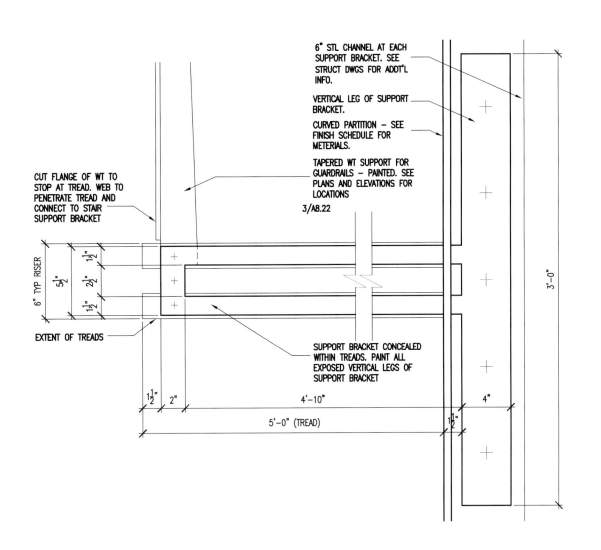

6" STL CHANNEL AT EACH
SUPPORT BRACKET. SEE
STRUCT DWGS FOR ADDT'L
INFO.

VERTICAL LEG OF SUPPORT
BRACKET.

CURVED PARTITION – SEE
FINISH SCHEDULE FOR
METERIALS.

TAPERED WT SUPPORT FOR
GUARDRAILS – PAINTED. SEE
PLANS AND ELEVATIONS FOR
LOCATIONS

3/A8.22

CUT FLANGE OF WT TO
STOP AT TREAD. WEB TO
PENETRATE TREAD AND
CONNECT TO STAIR
SUPPORT BRACKET

6" TYP RISER

5½"

1½"

2½"

1½"

EXTENT OF TREADS

SUPPORT BRACKET CONCEALED
WITHIN TREADS. PAINT ALL
EXPOSED VERTICAL LEGS OF
SUPPORT BRACKET

1½" 2" 4'-10" 4"

5'-0" (TREAD) 1½"

3'-0"

Architect: Dale Jones-Evans Pty Ltd Architecture   Photography: Giorgio Possenti, Jeremy Simons

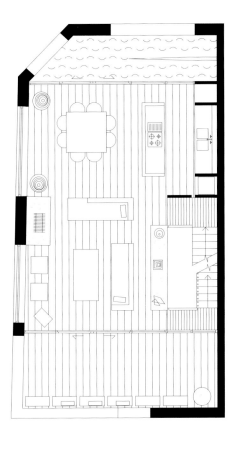

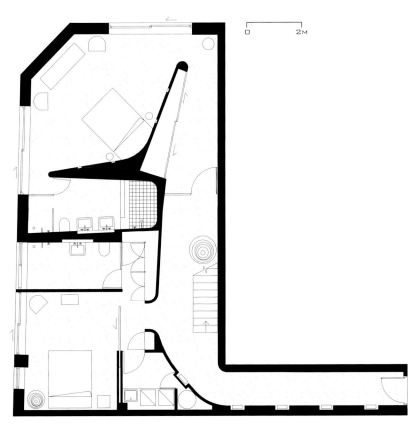

0   2M

Architect: Zimmer Gunsul Frasca Partnership   **Photography:** Eckert and Eckert

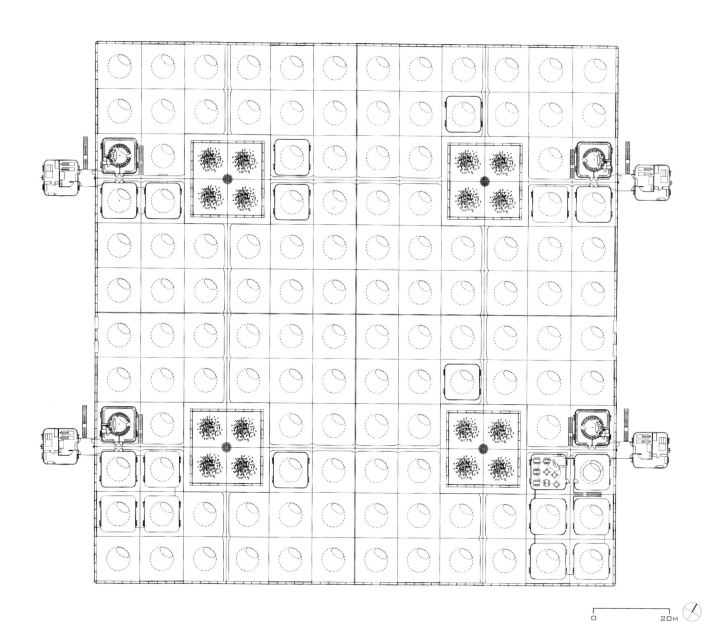

Architect: Nicholas Grimshaw & Partners   **Photography:** Tim Griffith

Architect: Suters Architects   **Photography**: Tyrone Branigan

IMAGES is pleased to add *Upstairs Downstairs* to its compendium of design and architectural publications.

We wish to thank all participating firms for their valuable contribution to this publication.

In particular, we would like to thank Sander Architects for allowing the use of their photograph on the cover of this book.

Special thanks is also extended to the late Eamonn McKenna (craftsman, Damien Murtagh Architects), for his contribution to *Upstairs Downstairs*.